ROUTLEDGE LIBRARY EDITIONS:
LIBRARY AND INFORMATION SCIENCE

Volume 12

BRITISH UNIVERSITY LIBRARIES

BRITISH UNIVERSITY LIBRARIES

TOBY BURROWS

Routledge
Taylor & Francis Group

LONDON AND NEW YORK

First published in 1989 by The Haworth Press, Inc.

This edition first published in 2020
by Routledge
2 Park Square, Milton Park, Abingdon, Oxon OX14 4RN

and by Routledge
52 Vanderbilt Avenue, New York, NY 10017

Routledge is an imprint of the Taylor & Francis Group, an informa business

© 1989 The Haworth Press, Inc.

All rights reserved. No part of this book may be reprinted or reproduced or utilised in any form or by any electronic, mechanical, or other means, now known or hereafter invented, including photocopying and recording, or in any information storage or retrieval system, without permission in writing from the publishers.

Trademark notice: Product or corporate names may be trademarks or registered trademarks, and are used only for identification and explanation without intent to infringe.

British Library Cataloguing in Publication Data
A catalogue record for this book is available from the British Library

ISBN: 978-0-367-34616-4 (Set)
ISBN: 978-0-429-34352-0 (Set) (ebk)
ISBN: 978-0-367-36129-7 (Volume 12) (hbk)
ISBN: 978-0-367-36133-4 (Volume 12) (pbk)
ISBN: 978-0-429-34407-7 (Volume 12) (ebk)

Publisher's Note
The publisher has gone to great lengths to ensure the quality of this reprint but points out that some imperfections in the original copies may be apparent.

Disclaimer
The publisher has made every effort to trace copyright holders and would welcome correspondence from those they have been unable to trace.

British University Libraries

Toby Burrows

The Haworth Press
New York • London

British University Libraries is #2 in the Haworth Series in Library and Information Science.

© 1989 by The Haworth Press, Inc. All rights reserved. No part of this work may be reproduced or utilized in any form or by any means, electronic or mechanical, including photocopying, microfilm and recording, or by any information storage and retrieval system, without permission in writing from the publisher. Printed in the United States of America.

The Haworth Press, Inc., 10 Alice Street, Binghamton, NY 13904-1580
EUROSPAN/Haworth, 3 Henrietta Street, London WC2E 8LU England

Library of Congress Cataloging-in-Publication Data

Burrows, Toby.
   British university libraries / Toby Burrows.
     p. cm. — (Haworth series in library and information science, ISSN 0897-8476 ; #2)
   Includes bibliographies and index.
   ISBN 0-86656-917-0
   1. Libraries, University and college—Great Britain. I. Title. II. Series.
Z675.U5B895 1989
027.70941—dc20
                                            89-2193
                                               CIP

CONTENTS

Acknowledgements	vii
List of Abbreviations	viii
Introduction	1
Chapter 1: The Universities	5
Chapter 2: Governance and Funding	21
Chapter 3: Staffing	45
Chapter 4: Collections	69
Chapter 5: Services and Buildings	95
Chapter 6: Automation	119
Chapter 7: Relations with Other Libraries	143
Conclusion	165
Index	173

Acknowledgements

The research for this book was undertaken during the academic year 1986/87, and was made possible by the award of the James Cook Bicentenary Scholarship. I am most grateful to the University of Western Australia and the University Librarian, Arthur Ellis, for granting me leave during this period. I am also indebted to University College London and Professor Andrew Watson, for appointing me to an Honorary Research Fellowship in the School of Library Archive and Information Studies for 1986/87.

Among the many people in Britain who deserve my thanks, I must single out James Thompson and Miles Blackwell for their helpfulness and encouragement, as well as the Chairman and Secretary of SCONUL for allowing me to attend the April 1987 meeting of SCONUL.

Above all, I am very grateful to the many library staff throughout Britain who were so helpful and hospitable, and gave generously of their time when they had little or none to spare. I hope they will forgive the temerity of an outsider in reducing the complexities of the real world to the generalizations of this book.

Some of the material in this book has previously appeared in the *Australian Library Journal* and the *British Journal of Academic Librarianship*. I thank the editors of these journals and their publishers (the Library Association of Australia and Taylor Graham, respectively) for permission to use this material here.

List of Abbreviations

AUT	Association of University Teachers
BCOP	Birmingham Libraries in Co-operation
BLAISE	British Library Automated Information Service
BLCMP	Birmingham Libraries Co-operative Mechanization Project
CLAIM	Centre for Library and Information Management
CURL	Consortium of University Research Libraries
CVCP	Committee of Vice-Chancellors and Principals
JANET	Joint Academic Network
LASER	London and South Eastern Library Region
LISC	Library and Information Services Council
LOCAS	Local Catalogue Service (British Library)
MARC	Machine-readable cataloguing
MOYUL	Meeting of Yorkshire University Librarians
OCLC	Online Computer Library Center
OPAC	On-line Public Access Catalogue
S_3RBK	Southampton, Surrey, Sussex, Reading, Brunel and Kent University libraries
REMARC	Retrospective Machine-readable cataloguing
SCOLCAP	Scottish Libraries Co-operative Automation Project
SCONUL	Standing Conference of National and University Libraries
SWALCAP	South Western Academic Libraries Co-operative Automation Project
UGC	University Grants Committee
UMIST	University of Manchester Institute of Science and Technology
UWIST	University of Wales Institute of Science and Technology

Introduction

British university libraries have begun to face major financial, technological, and organizational challenges. Cuts in funding, the spread of new technology, and changes to the provision of university education as a whole are combining to alter fundamentally the circumstances in which university libraries operate. As a result, the services they provide are being re-examined, from a need to manage with fewer resources as well as from a desire to improve the range and quality of services. The relative priority of collection-building compared with providing access to external resources is also being reconsidered. Automation, with its new possibilities and new requirements, is rapidly affecting all aspects of library activities. The way in which libraries are organized, especially in relation to financial management and administrative structures, is also being critically examined. As a result British university libraries in future decades will be very different from what they were in the recent past.

This book identifies the main trends which have emerged since July, 1981 when the government announced funding cuts for universities. It also tries to project these trends into the future and to assess their likely effect over the next few years. It is not an exhaustive catalogue of all the activities of university libraries, but concentrates instead on the most important developments in the areas of finance, staffing, collections, services, automation, and relations with other libraries. The changes affecting universities as a whole are also analyzed; these broad influences have been a major cause of change in university libraries and are essential to an understanding of that change.

Individual libraries are examined in relation to this general picture. A separate account and assessment of each library has not been given. Such judgments are largely subjective since there are no obvious independent criteria for measuring the quality of a university library. Individual assessments would also require more than a passing acquaintance with the library if they are to rise above mere impressions. In any case, a survey of individual libraries only stresses the differences between them. Such variations reveal far more about the local conditions and history of particular universities than they do about the essential nature of university libraries. It is the latter with which this book is concerned.

Nevertheless, the extent of differences between individual libraries is such that generalizations, especially statistical ones, must be made with caution. The statistics published by the Standing Conference for National and University Libraries (SCONUL) use two methods of grouping similar institutions. The first is by student numbers, while the second follows the classification devised by the Centre for Research in User Studies at the University of Sheffield: Oxbridge, London, Larger Civic, Smaller Civic, Ancient Scottish, Welsh, New, and Technological. These are of some use as a framework for discussions based on comparative statistics, but the statistics themselves are still unreliable and hard to compare, despite SCONUL's considerable efforts in the last few years.[1] Local factors, such as different loan periods or varying numbers of sites, have a hidden effect on financial and operational statistics alike. Ratios such as "staffing expenditure as a percentage of the library budget," or "expenditure per full-time-equivalent student," have so many local variations built into them that their use for comparison tends to be selective and political, not analytical. The comparison of ratios over several years for individual libraries is complicated by the difficulty of allowing for unique circumstances in particular years, especially during a period when university finances have been so volatile and variable. A further general complication is the difference between SCONUL's financial statistics and those of the UGC (University Grants Committee)[2]; they are compiled from different sources and on different bases, and cannot be compared.

An account of British university libraries in quantitative terms would rest, therefore, on a very uncertain and unstable statistical foundation. But the emphasis in this book is not on quantitative analysis. It focuses instead on an assessment of the essential and common qualitative characteristics of these libraries. In order for meaningful generalizations to be made, some boundaries have had to be drawn, and certain institutions have been regarded as falling outside the book's scope. Those which are highly specialized, such as the business schools and some of the London colleges and schools, have been excluded. So has the Open University, because its teaching methods are so different and it is not funded through the UGC. The Royal College of Art and the Cranfield Institute of Technology are also excluded, because of their specialization and their non-UGC funding. Buckingham, the only private university, has been included, but not in the discussion of funding.

The aim has been to use a definition of a university library which is more than just a nominal or administrative one, and which is linked to a definition of a university based on the range of its teaching, its size, and the source of its funds. Those institutions falling within the scope of this definition have common goals and activities sufficient to enable valid and worthwhile generalizations to be made about them. The libraries discussed in this book have their distinctive individual characters, but they are bound together by a whole range of shared aims and policies and by generally similar circumstances. It is these common and shared features of British university libraries which I attempt to show here.

REFERENCES

1. SCONUL. *University library expenditure statistics*, 1981/82– ; *SCONUL statistical database part II, library operations*, 1984/85– .
2. *University statistics, vol. 3, Finance*, 1980/81– .

Chapter 1

The Universities

In July, 1981, British universities were told by the University Grants Committee (UGC) what their individual allocations would be for the years 1981/82 to 1983/84. They had already been warned to expect cuts in their recurrent grants of at least 11%. The final cuts were unevenly distributed; some universities had their grant reduced by 40% or more, while others lost less than 5%. Salford, Aston, Bradford, and Keele were the worst affected, while Bath, Cambridge, and York were among those who were least affected. These reductions came soon after government policy on overseas students had been changed, requiring most students to pay the full cost of their education. This had caused a rapid decrease in the number of overseas students and in universities' income from them.

The effects of these cuts were drastic. Many courses were dropped—at least 250 in one estimate.[1] Departments were closed or merged. Economies were made in maintenance and running costs. Above all, staff were reduced. Over 7,000 staff (two-thirds of them academic) left under an early retirement scheme, at a cost of over £150 million. More than 10,000 jobs were lost altogether over the next four years.[2] Academic posts were reduced by one in seven.[3] These losses hit individual departments at random, with little regard for their overall balance, and stripped them of many of their most senior and experienced staff. The universities were left confused and demoralized in the face of substantial and rapid cuts which fell in an arbitrary and unplanned manner.

The government's contribution to planned change was to make extra money available for teaching and research in information technology, and to create 230 so-called "new blood" posts, mainly in science and technology. The UGC gave each university advice on which subjects to expand or close, and where to reduce or increase student numbers, but universities were free to ignore this advice, as quite a few did. Student numbers were held down overall, but the staff/student ratio gradually worsened. However, the cuts in income and staff, on the whole, did not fall in a planned way; their random and sudden nature greatly increased the universities' demoralization.

Not until May, 1985 did the government present its policies for the future development of the universities. But its Green Paper, *The development of higher education into the 1990s*, ignored several important issues and was limited to generalizations and exhortations in most of the topics covered. It predicted a 14% fall in full-time student numbers in the 1990s, and urged selectivity in research, greater accountability and better management, and closer links with industry and commerce. It stressed the role of the universities in producing qualified manpower necessary for economic growth. It made no mention of future levels of funding or of staffing levels.

However, the UGC's planning document, issued in September, 1984, concentrated on these subjects. It argued for increases in the level of recurrent, equipment, and capital grants and warned of "further disruption and decline" otherwise.[5] It rejected the possibility of more reductions in staff without considerable special funding. Like the Green Paper, it recommended more selective research and better management, and it foreshadowed a new method of allocating grants to individual universities.

In its January, 1986 response, the Committee of Vice-Chancellors and Principals (CVCP) attacked the Green Paper as "blinkered" and inadequate.[6] It rejected the projected fall in student numbers, and recounted the universities' efforts toward the general goals set out in the Green Paper. Above all, it emphasized that funding was the central issue. The cuts in recurrent income had caused considerable damage and severe suffering; further cuts would be a disaster and would "put everything we do into jeopardy."[7] In addition, research funds, equipment funds, and capital grants were all far too low, the CVCP said. It also listed the many difficulties caused by reduced staffing.

This CVCP response drew heavily on the March, 1985 report of its Steering Committee for Efficiency Studies in Universities, chaired by Sir Alex Jarratt. The Jarratt Report was based on a study of management structures and administrative systems at six universities. It recommended far-reaching changes to the way in which universities were organized and managed, and especially in their methods of allocating resources within the university. It looked in detail at questions of accountability and performance indicators, and at planning horizons. The level of government funding for universities and the way in which funds were distributed were also considered. The need for universities to adapt to sweeping changes was emphasized. The Jarratt Report itself was an integral part of these changes, and met a mixed reception within the universities as a result. But it gave the CVCP a blueprint for meeting government expectations of structural change in universities, and its recommendations are being widely implemented, with government and CVCP backing.

A fundamental change has also taken place in the method used by the UGC to allocate grants to individual universities. From 1986/87, block grants have been distributed according to a formula with separate components for teaching and research. The teaching part of the grant, (61.2%) is based on student numbers, using a national "unit level of resource" for each student which varies according to the nature of different subjects. The research part (34.8%) is based on the UGC's assessment of the standard of research work in individual subjects at each university. These research rankings were announced in May, 1986, and are expected to be reviewed after five years. They graded research in five categories, from outstanding to poor. Though the methodology was dubious and the criteria too subjective, the rankings were generally tolerated. For every department or university which complained that it had been unfairly treated, there was another which took pride in the fact that it had done well. The remaining 4% of the block grant is for "special factors."

The formula has allowed the UGC to shift money to those universities with the best research ratings, and to tie teaching funds closely to its own estimate of student numbers in particular subjects at individual universities. There was an immediate effect on the relative fortunes of groups of universities, with some receiving increased funding in real terms and others being cut. For the first two years of the new funding formula, a so-called "safety net" was used to lessen the variation between universities. In 1986/87, no university was allowed to be more than 1.5% worse off than the average; eleven institutions ended up in this position, which meant a cut of 0.5% compared with an average increase of 1%. In 1987/88, the safety net was lowered to 2.5%; it applied to eight institutions, which received a rise of 0.7%, compared with the average of 3.2%. Bangor, Aberdeen, Dundee, Durham, East Anglia, and Keele were in the safety net for both years. The increases for the most successful universities under the formula were restricted, to provide funds for the safety net. Nevertheless, in 1987/88, Warwick and York were allocated an increase of 6.4% in cash terms, twice the average. In 1988/89, the average rise was 3.2% again, but the safety net was abandoned.

The UGC itself also faced fundamental change. The report in February, 1987 of a review committee chaired by Lord Croham recommended that the UGC be renamed the University Grants Council, become part of the machinery of government, and include members from outside the academic world. The trend toward selectivity was strongly endorsed, and a three-year funding cycle was suggested.[8] Most of the Croham Report's basic ideas were adopted by the government in its White Paper on higher education, issued in April, 1987.

The government proposed a Universities Funding Council, establishing by legislation and part of public administration, with greater representation from industry and commerce, and an improved secretariat and simplified structure. The Council would make contracts with universities rather than allocate grants to them, but would not be given three-year funding. The White Paper also restated government policy toward the universities. It asked universities for greater control of quality and standards, for measurements of efficiency and effectiveness, and for continued changes in management and organization. It gave projections for increased recurrent grants to 1989/90 at an average rate of about 5% a year, and it predicted a greater rise in student numbers to 1990 and a smaller decrease between 1990 and 1996 than the figures in the Green Paper had suggested. The emphasis remained on the role of higher education in serving the "economic requirements of the country."[9] Despite its much more elaborate and glossy format and its proposals for altering the UGC, the White Paper differed little from the earlier, and much-criticized, Green Paper in its general tone and approach.

British universities, then, are in the midst of profound changes in the way they are organized and managed, the way funds are distributed to them, and the way in which they serve society and account to it for their activities. This change is now being given direction by the government, the UGC, and the universities themselves, in contrast to times when financial crisis was the major agent of change. But the financial pressures have not gone away, and for many universities they have grown more acute, as the cumulative effect of several years of expenditure exceeding income takes effect. Most universities are faced with accumulating deficits of considerable proportions, which will increase if further economies are not made. Another period of closures and mergers of departments and reductions in staff has already begun, with thousands more academic posts likely to be lost. The larger civic universities like Birmingham, Leeds, and Sheffield are among those making substantial reductions in staff. Oxford University has planned for an 11% cut between 1986/87 and 1990/91, with a loss of 190 academic staff. Universities in the UGC safety net, like Aberdeen, have been badly affected, while University College Cardiff brought itself to the brink of closure by a combination of reduced funding, financial mismanagement, and overambitious subject coverage. In general, those universities which have tried to preserve teaching and research in a broad range of subjects while ignoring UGC recommendations for selectivity are now faced with substantial deficits. The new round of cuts has been caused as much by these deficits as by continuing cuts in recurrent grants in real terms.

These cuts differ from those of the earlier 1980s in that a framework for planning is now available, however unpalatable it may be to many institutions. The universities are reshaping themselves, with varying degrees of reluctance, along the lines set out by the government and the UGC: greater selectivity, rationalization, closure of small departments, improved standards and accountability, and better management and organization. It is no exaggeration to regard this as the most dramatic change to the universities in over 20 years, and probably the most drastic restructuring ever. This is the context in which British university libraries now have to operate, and they too will be greatly affected by these changes. For this reason, it is important to look in some detail at the major elements in this restructuring of the universities.

At the broadest level, the government and the universities hold differing views about the aims and objectives of higher education. The Jarratt Report repeated the aims defined in 1963 by the Robbins Committee as the basis for the rapid expansion of university education in the 1960s: instruction in skills, the promotion of the general powers of the mind, the advancement of learning, and the transmission of a common culture and common standards of citizenship. The government White Paper also quoted the Robbins definitions, but made it clear that its emphasis was very different. Universities should aim, above all, to serve the economic requirements of the country and to be more relevant to industry and commerce and enterprise in general. This is not the only aim of higher education, according to the White Paper, but it is certainly the most important one and the one which underlies government policy toward universities. Neither the CVCP nor the UGC commented on the government's view in their major advice on planning and funding. The Jarratt Report repeated the Robbins definitions, but did not discuss the question of aims and objectives any further. Despite widespread disagreement with the government's views on universities, the official statements of university and UGC policy have let those views prevail by default and have concentrated on their practical effects instead.

The UGC and CVCP, for all their warnings of disaster and collapse, have kept well away from the all-out confrontation with the government which might well result from open disagreements about basic objectives. In such a confrontation the universities would be the only losers, since the government has proved itself willing to make sharp cuts in funding even without such confrontation. Nor would there be much public support for the universities. The CVCP's response to the Green Paper finished with a reminder that the priority and level of resources for higher education were questions to be decided by the electorate. Unfortunately for the universities, the government's views are much more likely to prevail with the electorate. Too many people, of all political parties, have little or no sympathy for the universities. They are either elitist and over-privileged, or parasitic and cut off from the real world of enterprise, depending on one's political point of view. The Conservative journalist Paul Johnson accused the universities of "whining mendicancy and malevolent parasitism," and attacked academics for insisting that "the country owes them a comfortable living while teaching the young to look down on those who provide it"; in his view, "the universities must be required to work for their survival."[10]

In this unsympathetic climate, the universities have had little choice but to change themselves along the lines set out by the government. One of the most important of these changes has been the emphasis on selectivity and rationalization. The UGC has pursued a policy of selective funding for research, and has advised individual universities to discontinue teaching in some subjects and to expand their activities in others. The aim has been to concentrate teaching and research in most subjects at fewer universities than before, and on a larger scale than before at each of these. At Exeter, for example, the Department of Philosophy was being closed, and one staff member transferred to Nottingham. The university received staff in Italian, Russian, drama, and theology transferred from other institutions. The Department of Computer Science and the School of Education are undergoing considerable expansion. Sheffield lost classics and Italian, but is expanding in electronic and control engineering. This rationalization is also occurring at smaller universities like Bradford, heavily cut in 1981, and now further reducing its work in mechanical engineering and chemistry while expanding in electrical and civil engineering, environmental sciences, and management. In general, the shift has been toward technological and commercial subjects, and away from the arts.

Parallel to this selectivity and rationalization of subjects offered is a move toward reorganizing departmental structures. Hull is replacing its departments with 11 schools; City University and Sheffield are also combining some of their departments into schools. Some universities, like Bath, have always had a structure based on schools rather than departments, and this type of organization is being increasingly used as a means of retaining a broader subject coverage than would be possible with separate departments for each subject. Traditional university structures are also being weakened by the continuing proliferation of centres and institutes, designed to take advantage of earmarked grants and research contracts in specific areas. In future, more universities will be organized into larger subject groups, with the more specific centres and institutes attached to them. But the result of this reorganization remains, for most universities, a narrower range of subjects taught and researched, with some areas dropped and others expanded.

Also emerging is a restructuring of universities' internal financial management and decision making. This is occurring within the framework established by the Jarratt Report; the government, the UGC, and the CVCP are all expecting universities to implement the recommendations made in the report, and funding is gradually becoming linked to progress in doing so. The Jarratt framework includes a much more active role for the Court (or governing body), which should draw many of its members from outside the university. The influence and role of the Senate (or large academic representative body) should be reduced and delegated. The vice-chancellor (or principal) and the heads of departments or schools should be managers and leaders with greater executive power than before, and should be appointed by the Court or governing body. The many committees existing in universities should be frequently reviewed and pruned; they should be fewer and smaller, take up less of their members' time, and delegate on routine matters. Allocation of resources and planning, which were often fragmented between several committees and poorly coordinated, should be the responsibility of a single, small committee.

Almost all universities are changing themselves along these lines. Many have set up a Planning and Resources Committee or Academic Planning Committee of the type recommended by the Jarratt Report. Committees everywhere have been reviewed, revised, and abolished. Councils and vice-chancellors alike are acquiring greater formal powers for running the universities. The UGC has monitored responses to the Jarratt report and plans to publish an account of these in each university. The administrative structure emerging from the implementation of the Jarratt Report's recommendations differs considerably from past structures. Academics have tended to prefer a collegial-type organization, in which hierarchy is minimized and as many staff as possible have a say in decision making. The best-known example of this is, of course, Oxford University where the body consisting of all the Masters of Arts (Convocation) has the final say, though this is exercised only occasionally. Opponents of the Jarratt Report have argued that a move toward greater hierarchy and centralization will damage the intellectual freedom of individual academics, which the traditional looser structure centred on the Senate was intended to protect.

There are areas, however, in which the Jarratt recommendations work toward devolution rather than centralization. Many universities are now reorganizing their financial management so that individual departments become cost centres or budget centres, with a single budget figure to allocate among staff, materials, and overheads like electricity and telephone charges. Heads of departments have greater responsibility for determining specific priorities and levels of expenditure, within the university's overall planning and expenditure guidelines. Centralization can also be softened by regular rotation of senior posts like Pro-Vice-Chancellor, as happens at Southampton. Nevertheless, the trend is very much to concentrate planning and decision making, while giving departments greater responsibility for controlling expenditure of their allocation. Universities are coming to resemble large companies or government agencies more than loose associations of teachers and researchers.

It remains to be seen whether this process will damage intellectual freedom or reduce the contribution of universities to the goals set out by the Robbins Committee. The universities are convinced they have no choice but to go in the direction recommended by the government and the Jarratt Report. Without government funding, British universities could not remain the same; with government funding, they must change as well. The type of university molded by the government's policies is increasingly similar to privately funded universities, so far represented only on a small scale in Britain by the University of Buckingham, now with a royal charter and a seat on the CVCP. This convergence of public and private universities leaves those funded by the government without the choice of maintaining their traditional organization and structure.

A further clear indication of this convergence is the increasing emphasis by universities on raising funds from sources outside the UGC and fees for home students. The Government White Paper estimated that 33% of university income came from these sources in

1984/85, compared with 24% in 1980/81, and the universities are making considerable efforts to increase the percentage further. Overseas students are growing in numbers again, after the sharp fall when full fees were introduced in 1980. Many institutions are mounting strong recruiting campaigns, in the Middle East and Southeast Asia especially. International links with overseas universities are being encouraged as a way of attracting more overseas students and visitors. Courses are more likely to be tailored or developed with the interests of overseas students in mind. North American students are being urged to spend their junior year abroad in specific British universities. Other fee-paying students outside the UGC structure are being sought; self-financing courses in continuing and vocational education and summer schools are two of the main avenues.

The other main source of non-UGC funds is from closer links with industry and commerce. Much greater efforts are being made to win research contracts from commercial sources. Over 30 science parks have been established to promote local economic development and better research links between universities and industry. Some of these have been able to attract funding from local authorities, and most have grown rapidly with successful tenants. But a few have had problems with limits to the extent to which universities can control the development of the science park.[11] A major reason for establishing these parks has been to help market universities' innovations in science and technology, often through university companies. Almost all universities now have several companies to market innovations. City University, for example, owns City Technology Limited, which markets electrochemical gas sensors, and Citifluor Limited, marketing mountant solutions for microscopy. Sheffield University has seven companies under the control of its own holding company, Unisheff Ventures Limited; they market products in fields like biotechnology, computer-aided design, and medical physics. These commercial activities, frequently housed at science parks, are an important means of bringing university innovations to the attention of industry and commerce, and of earning non-UGC income for the universities.

They are also part of a wider process linking universities more closely with society at large. Closer relations with industry and commerce are paralleled by a greater involvement in the local community through community education programmes, public events, and greater contact with schools. Universities are advertising and marketing themselves much more than before, and publicity about the university is becoming a major activity. Added to this are numerous conferences, exhibitions, and the like held at universities. Involvement with the world outside the university even extends to promoting student halls of residence as holiday flats during the summer vacation. The popular picture of universities used to regard them as inward-looking and isolated from the rest of society, but universities are now making strenuous effects to show that this is false. Closer links with industry and commerce and with the local community are complemented by increased involvement in university governance by people from outside the university. While the universities are expanding their interest in the outside world, they are also looking more closely at what goes on inside.

A major part of this closer look has been a demand for greater accountability. The 1985 Green Paper asked for the setting and monitoring of general academic standards, and the development and use of performance measures. The White Paper took the same line. The CVCP's response, in the area of standards, has been to prepare codes of "best practice" for external examiners, postgraduate training and research, and the training and development of academic staff. It has drawn up guidelines for appraisal and assessment of academic and academic-related staff, though few universities have yet implemented them. The CVCP is also working to produce measures of performance which are acceptable to the government. The Green Paper saw this in terms of cost-benefit analysis and value for money, and wanted to concentrate on measuring the output of qualified manpower and ignore other, less tangible benefits. Both the Green Paper and the Jarratt Report provided lists of possible measures relevant to these aims. The CVCP and the UGC agreed to issue a range of measures for each university from 1987. These will include such "efficiency indicators" as staff/student ratios and unit costs for the main categories of expenditure. There will also be "effectiveness indicators" such as income from research grants and contracts, numbers of research and sponsored students, submission rates for research degrees, first occupation of graduates, and contribution to postgraduate and professional training.[12] These measures are very similar to those proposed in the Green Paper and the Jarratt

Report, although Jarratt in particular also suggested a further group of measures for staff workloads, class sizes, course options, teaching quality, and availability of library stock and computing facilities. How the published measurements for each university will be assessed and used remains to be seen, but there will doubtless be pressure from the government to link them to the formula for distributing block grants to individual institutions.

Accountability will mean a much closer scrutiny of each member of staff, as well as each university. But this is only one of a series of major changes and difficulties affecting staff in universities. The cuts in staff numbers in the recent past were largely carried out in a random and unplanned way. The cuts of the future are intended to be planned and costed in detail before the UGC will allocate special funds for early retirement schemes. No university has yet resorted to compulsory redundancies, though some have considered this very carefully. Tenure for life made it unlikely that sacking university staff could be upheld by the courts. The government has announced that it will legislate to end tenure for all new appointments, and some institutions are already appointing new staff to renewable contracts instead of to permanent tenure.

With the early retirement schemes and reduction in numbers of posts, the universities have lost many of their older and more experienced staff. But they have also been unable to recruit new staff, and a whole generation of young potential academics has been lost. Many universities are finding themselves with an "age profile" (or distribution of staff by age) which is disproportionately heavy for the 35 to 49-year-old group. The UGC suggested that the ideal should be 40% of staff in this age group, with a further 40% over 49 and 20% under 35. But it estimated that the average for all universities was 57% of staff aged between 35 and 49, with 17% under 35 and 26% over 49.[13] This covers considerable variations among universities, depending on when they were last able to recruit significant numbers of new staff. At Sheffield, for example, 25% of staff were under 35 in 1979/80; by 1986/87, the proportion had fallen to 16%. The 35 to 49 age group increased from 55 to 58%, and those over 49 increased from 20% to 26%.[14] Many universities now recognize this problem, but there is little they can do to change the situation. Because the total number of staff is still shrinking, there will not be vacant posts to be filled after further early retirements take place. Only the creation of new posts in areas like electronic engineering and computer science, as a result of earmarked and selective funding, will enable more than a trickle of young academics to be appointed. The disproportionate numbers of staff aged between 35 and 49 will continue to grow.

Recruitment and retention of staff, especially in the favoured technological and commercial subjects, has been hampered by increasingly inadequate salary scales. Poor salaries have also been a major obstacle to reviving staff morale in a period of continuing cuts and rapid change. In early 1987, the government and the Universities Academic Salaries Committees (representing the universities and the Association of University Teachers [AUT]) reached an agreement on pay rises after a lengthy and often bitter dispute, which included a half-day strike — the first ever in the universities — in January 1986. In exchange for an increase of 24% spread over two financial years, the AUT and the vice-chancellors agreed to government demands for improving methods of promotion, probation, and appraisal. The lecturer scale was divided into two grades, with promotion depending on satisfactory performance. Promotion to senior lecturer was also made dependent upon merit and appraisal, not length of service. The ratio of senior staff (professors and senior lecturers), which had been set nationally at 40%, became the responsibility of each university, to be decided within the limits imposed by its available funds. This, together with revised salary points on the new scales, was intended to allow universities much greater flexibility in rewarding their best staff with promotion and more substantial increments. But, on its own, the new salaries structure can do little to halt the departures for North America of talented academics in a wide range of subjects, or to restore the morale of those who remain.

Change is also affecting the student population of the universities, and is likely to accelerate in the next few years. The majority of students are still in the 18 to 24 age group, study full-time, and are supported by grants paid by local authorities. But the trend is away from this homogeneity. Overseas student numbers are growing again after a sudden fall caused by the introduction of full fees in 1980. Universities are trying to attract more part-time and mature-entry students, as well as more home students paying their own fees or being sponsored to study. The government's White Paper predicted a rise of 5% in total student numbers by 1990, followed by a decrease of about the same size between 1990 and 1996. A continuing fall in the size of the 18 and 19-year-old group as a whole would be compensated for by higher participation rates of that group in higher education and by a continuing rise in the proportion of mature-age new students, often with entrance qualifications different from the standard A-levels. The student population will become increasingly more varied; there will be a greater proportion of older students, part-time students, and overseas students. It is possible that a loans scheme may replace grants as the normal funding for home students. Universities will need to reorganize their courses and services to respond better to the requirements of an increasingly varied student population.

The government's forecast for student numbers is the only area where it has been willing to predict the future beyond the next financial year. The recent sudden cuts and crises have led to repeated calls from the universities and the UGC for longer "planning horizons." The Jarratt and Croham committees also recommended that the universities be given a much clearer picture of future funding levels to enable them to plan with greater confidence. But the White Paper rejected this, saying that it would be "undesirable to insulate university management from the need to plan for changing circumstances."[15] In effect, the government denied any essential difference between the requirements of university planning and those of civil service planning. Nevertheless, all universities have been asked by the UGC to prepare academic and financial plans for the period to 1990/91, covering research, staff, students, resources, subject coverage, and financial forecasts. Extra funds for restructuring and rationalization are dependent on the production of a satisfactory plan, which will no doubt also contribute to the UGC's assessment of individual universities for determining their block grants.

Completed plans vary somewhat in scope and detail. Many universities found it difficult to draw up a strategic plan with so little idea of likely funding levels for the period in question. But a comprehensive plan, like that produced by the University of Sheffield, is a valuable summary of all the current major trends in universities. The Sheffield plan, titled *A future for excellence*, has as its financial goals reducing dependence on the UGC's block recurrent grant, moving to a system of cost-centre budgeting, and allocating overheads to cost centres. Management and decision making are to be more streamlined, with fewer, smaller committees and greater executive power for heads of cost centres. Staff numbers will be voluntarily reduced, and there will be a rationalization of subjects taught and departmental organization. A Technology Park will be established, and closer outside links developed at the local, national, and international levels. There will be increased numbers of overseas, part-time, and mature-entry students, and continuing education will be stressed.

British universities of the coming decades will be markedly different from the traditional institutions. They will be organized and managed differently, with fewer staff and a changing student population. Their subject coverage will be much more selective, and will put more emphasis on science, technology, and commercial subjects. They will be more overtly organized to bid for research contracts and to establish links with industry. The overall system for allocating government funds will also be quite different. Such wide and varied change has already had a fundamental effect on the university libraries, too.

REFERENCES

1. Kogan, Maurice. *The attack on higher education* (London: Kogan Page, 1983), p. 12.
2. *Ibid.*, p. 11; *The Independent*, 5 November 1986.
3. *The development of higher education into the 1990s* (London: H.M.S.O., 1985), 9.1.
4. *Ibid.*, 9.2.
5. University Grants Committee. *A strategy for higher education into the 1990s* (London: H.M.S.O., 1984), 11.21.
6. Committee of Vice-Chancellors and Principals. *The future of the universities* (London: CVCP, 1986), 1.4.
7. *Ibid.*, 6.1.
8. *Review of the University Grants Committee* (London: H.M.S.O., 1987) (Cm. 81).

9. *Higher education: Meeting the challenge* (London: H.M.S.O., 1987) (Cm. 114), 1.4.
10. *Daily Telegraph*, 7 January 1987, p. 10.
11. *Times Higher Education Supplement*, 30 January 1987, p. 10.
12. *Higher education: Meeting the challenge*, 3.27.
13. *A strategy for higher education into the 1990s*, 7.2, 7.6-7.8.
14. University of Sheffield. *A future for excellence: strategic plan for 1990/91 and beyond* (1987), p. 6.
15. *Higher education: Meeting the challenge*, 4.42.

Chapter 2

Governance and Funding

The rapid and profound changes in British universities have been a forceful reminder that university libraries are inextricably linked to the fortunes of their parent institutions. In better times, there is often a tendency to take the university as a constant, and to disregard it as a cause of major change in university libraries. In Allen Veaner's assessment of the future for American academic libraries, for example, there is hardly any consideration of the potential effect of changes in the organization and funding of universities.[1] Events in Britain have shown all too clearly that such complacency is impossible. The universities are in the middle of drastic changes to the way in which they are funded, make decisions, and organize themselves, and their libraries cannot avoid being involved in this process.

The effects of these changes are being felt most in the areas of budgeting and finance, and in formal links with universities' decision-making structures. From this level they filter down to the whole of the library's day-to-day services and operations, since what a library can provide for its users and the methods it uses are largely constrained by the framework of funding and decision making within which it operates. There are other major forces for change at the operational level, notably new technology, but their importance is moulded and limited by this framework. British university libraries can no longer regard the framework as essentially constant and unchanging. It is changing fundamentally and quickly, and drastically altering the context of library activities.

Until recently almost all libraries were linked to their university by a Library Committee. These committees varied somewhat in membership and powers, but the general picture was fairly consistent, at least in England and Wales. The typical Library Committee was quite large, with 15 to 20 members, and met comparatively infrequently, usually once a term. The membership often included student representatives, as well as elected representatives of library staff. The academic members were sometimes chosen to represent each faculty or school, but the committee was equally likely to be a group of individuals with a general interest in library matters rather than with a specific constituency to represent. Sometimes the committee included one of the university's senior academic officials, usually as chairman ex officio; a Pro-Vice-Chancellor as chairman of the Library Committee could, in theory at least, be the library's voice in key decision-making bodies. In practice, however, the Library Committee often counted for very little in university politics. Its members were not influential enough and its powers were too limited. Its normal role was to advise the librarian and the Senate on library policy. It might consider and transmit the librarian's budget estimates, and look at the budget allocation, but did not usually make major changes even if it had the theoretical power to do so. A case of the Library Committee overruling the librarian on plans to make savings, as happened in one university during the 1981 cuts, was exceptional. Frequently, the librarian acted as secretary to the committee and could control its agenda and business. Its main function was as a sounding-board, enabling the library and the university to communicate with each other about developments affecting the library.

In Scotland, the picture was different. Most Library Committees played a more active and executive role, with greater control of finances and decision making. The librarian was usually responsible to the committee for the running of the library, instead of to the Vice-Chancellor or Principal as was usual in England and Wales. A stronger library committee meant less freedom of action for the librarian, but the corollary was greater formal support for the library within the university's decision making structure.

In some British universities, the Library Committee still survives unchanged, but in most the effects of the Jarratt recommendations are now being felt. Library Committees have not escaped the general review of university committees which began in 1985/86. Indeed, their size and infrequent meetings single them out for critical scrutiny. So does their usual link to the Senate (or large, representative academic committee), at a time when it is losing its power to small planning committees and to the Council or governing body with lay membership. Their comparative powerlessness also makes them often irrelevant to the routes by which the university makes decisions and allocates resources.

The abolition of the Library Committee is one possible reaction by the university. At Liverpool, the Library Committee was one of three committees merged to form a new Academic Services Sub-Committee, which is small and non-representative and reports to the influential Planning and Resources Committee. With a single committee to handle policy and resource allocation for the library, computing service, and media services, the amount of library-related committee business is greatly reduced and the library is in direct contact with the main decision-making channels. The price is the loss of separate consideration for the library, and the possibility in the future of having to compete with the other services for a fair share of the single allocation made to the Sub-Committee.

A less drastic reaction by the university is to turn the Library Committee into an advisory board or consultative committee answering to the central planning committee. At York, this has meant making the Library Committee a sub-committee of the central planning committee, drawing the library closer to the centre of decision making. Elsewhere, the membership of the Library Committee has been altered to include representatives of the committee controlling planning and allocation of resources. For a few libraries which already have a sub-committee of their Library Committee to deal with resources and finance (such as Edinburgh and Sheffield), it seems likely that this sub-committee will replace the main committee eventually and will be integrated into the university's resource allocation procedures.

The main function of the Library Committee in this new kind of structure is to provide advice from the librarian and academic staff on the library's needs for resources and to act as a channel for library submissions on budgets and planning. Without such a structure, the library will lose its links to decision making committees. At Leeds, for example, the creation of a Planning and Resources Committee meant that the librarian and the chairman of the Library

Committee lost their previous direct access to the Senate Planning Committee. At Sussex, where there has never been a Library Committee, the librarian's ex officio place on the earlier, large Planning Committee was not carried over to the new, smaller Planning Committee. For the library to be properly represented in the new, post-Jarratt management of universities, there must be a formal and direct line of communication between the library and the committee with responsibility for planning and resource allocation. Local conditions will decide whether this is as part of a services committee or as a separate committee for the library. But the library which is still tied to a pre-Jarratt Library Committee will have to rely on personal and informal contact for its links to decision-making committees and officials, and will be in a much weaker position.

Most Library Committees in the past dealt with advice from the librarian and advice to the librarian. Under the Jarratt recommendations, advice from the librarian is being integrated into university resource allocation structures. But advice *to* the librarian from the library's users falls outside Jarratt's scope. The librarian, like heads of departments, is regarded as the chief executive of the library, with full responsibility for decision making and management within the financial and planning framework established by the university. There is no obligation for the librarian to consult others and take their advice. Nevertheless, all librarians recognize the need to have a formal means of consulting the library's users, to explain library policy and developments, hear users' views of library services, and gain backing among the university community on specific issues. In future, this will have to be done separately from the formal resource allocation committee.

Even before the changes resulting from the Jarratt recommendations, many libraries had found that a single Library Committee could not adequately handle resources as well as consultation with users. In some cases this has meant a sub-committee to handle budgeting, as at Aston and Newcastle. But more frequently the result has been one or more separate committees of library users. Bath, for example, has a Library Liaison Committee composed of student representatives, academics representing each school of study, and all the subject librarians. The chairman is a member ex officio of the Library Committee, which has a much narrower membership and deals with policy matters. Kent and Stirling also have a Library Users Group as well as a Library Committee. At Sussex there is no Library Committee, but the librarian is required to convene and chair a consultative group of academics and students once a term.

Even more common is a system of Faculty Library Committees, as at Reading, Edinburgh, and the Bodleian. These may be part of the faculty rather than the library and are not always closely linked to the Library Committee, but they provide a formal channel of communication between the library and its users. At Liverpool, the Faculty Library Committees used to have representatives on the Library Committee; when it was abolished, communication with the faculties became much more difficult. A few libraries, notably Cambridge, Durham, and Reading, also have a separate committee for student users, who are otherwise not represented on library committees there.

Whether an elaborate system of user committees is necessary depends on local circumstances. But it is generally true that some form of user committee is essential if the library is to be seen as trying to respond to its users' needs. So, at a time when the Library Committee is becoming part of the resource allocation structure or even being abolished as a separate entity, the library must ensure that adequate provision for consultation with users exists or is created as a specific body. Clearly, one consequence of the Jarratt recommendations is that resource and policy matters should no longer be dealt with in the same committee that examines advice from library users.

In the midst of these changes, it will be some time before the extent of the librarian's ability to influence university decision making is clear. In the meantime, personal contacts with influential academics and administrators are more important than ever. An even greater proportion of the chief librarian's time is spent presenting the library's case informally as well as formally to the university. Much depends on the librarian's personality and ability to create a climate of opinion favourable to the library. There are many ways of doing this. At Sheffield, senior financial officials were given a behind the scenes tour of the library, including the chance to use online financial databases. At Exeter, a series of seminars was held to explain developments in information technology to academic staff. No doubt there are risks in this kind of initiative; the library may damage itself by a poor performance on these occasions and the visitors may draw the wrong conclusions about library needs. But the risk needs to be taken, since the senior academics and administrators who control decision making are rarely frequent users of the library. They should be encouraged to understand how the library works and what constraints there are on its services. This is not marketing in the commercial sense; it is a pragmatic response to changing decision-making structures in universities. None of the new central planning and resources committees seems to have a librarian on it ex officio, so it is vital for the library to have direct, informal contact with members of such committees and with the administrative staff who control the implementation of committee decisions.

This is particularly evident in the case of library budgets. Many libraries are no longer asked to submit formal estimates of their financial needs for the next year. They are simply informed of their budget after the university has been through its procedures for allocating resources. Some have informal discussions with a senior financial official before the budget is finalized, but this is to negotiate the details, not to decide the overall amount. Those libraries which submit estimates, normally through the Library Committee, describe the procedure as farcical, since these estimates are usually ignored and the budget decided along completely different lines. For many libraries, the university calculates the likely staff expenditure and adds an amount for non-staff expenditure which includes a small percentage increase consistent with any rise in the university's overall grant. The amount therefore bears no relation to what the library considers it needs, nor to inflation rates for library materials. The budget is communicated to the library by the Finance Officer or Bursar. it is no wonder, then, that many librarians are convinced that this official is the real arbiter of the library budget.

In recent years, the budget is much more likely to have been calculated on the basis of a percentage reduction or target savings. Few libraries were in the position of University College London and the Bodleian, which had some indexation for rising costs of library materials built into their budget. Most budgets continue to be historically based, with the previous year's budget given a percentage increase or decrease. Some libraries, like Newcastle and Aberystwyth, are given a fixed percentage of the university or college's income. University College London has its budget derived from the College's by a formula. In these cases, the library's budget is linked directly to the overall financial position of the parent institution, whereas in historically based budgets, it is possible for the library to be treated more favourably or less favourably than the rest of the university. Few libraries have been asked to undertake zero-base budgeting; Aston experimented with it briefly, and the City University asked all departments to use it in 1986/87. In the future, there may be growth in allocation by formula or percentage, but the historically based budget will still be used for most libraries.

There will certainly be growth in the number of libraries given one-line budgets. Some libraries, such as Keele, Newcastle, Sheffield, and several London colleges, are already in the position of being given a single amount for staff, materials, and running costs. In a few cases, this type of budget includes a limitation on the maximum percentage which can be spent on staff. The division of the single sum among the various expenditure heads is done by the librarian and presented to the Library Committee for comment and advice. Most librarians have welcomed the flexibility which the one-line budget provides. The librarian can respond to changing circumstances more quickly and easily, especially as there is usually also virement between budget heads after the division has been made. There is greater scope for using staff savings to improve other areas of expenditure in times of cuts and target savings. Several librarians have followed a policy of protecting expenditure on materials by keeping staff levels comparatively low. But the one-line budget also means greater responsibility and pressure on the librarian. Academics may well claim that the librarian is spending too much on staff, even when most staff are permanent and academic-related staff have just received a large increase in salary. With a one-line budget, the librarian is taking on responsibility for setting the staff establishment, usually set by the university in the past. Under the Jarratt recommendations, this is precisely what a head of department is expected to do, as part of his role as chief executive. In the next few years, many more librarians will be expected to work with a one-line budget, with its mixture of added benefits and pressures.

The key to the one-line budget is the inclusion of expenditure on staff. Some libraries already have a single grant for non-staff purposes. This is then divided between appropriate heads, usually by the librarian who presents the figures to the Library Committee for comment. In most Scottish libraries, the Library Committee decides the division, on the advice of the librarian. The amount of flexibility available under this method is quite limited, since most of the budget is allocated to materials. Staffing expenditure remains outside the librarian's control, in a separate budget calculated by the university. This arrangement is little different in practice from a budget which comes to the librarian already divided up into several categories. This is very common, though local circumstances determine the number and narrowness of these categories. In its simplest form, this type of budget contains one sum for materials (books, periodicals, and binding) and another for other expenses (such as automation, stationery, inter-library loans, and so on). At its most complex, the same type of budget can be divided into many detailed heads. Cambridge and the Bodleian both have budget estimates like this, under general headings for staff, materials, administration, and premises, each divided into several sub-categories. Many other libraries fall somewhere in between. But without a budget with staffing costs included and full virement there is only a marginal gain in flexibility available from different forms and methods of dividing the budget. Cuts and target savings are difficult to make. The Library Committee or the university's financial officials may force the librarian to make reductions in what are, from the library's point of view, the wrong areas of the budget. With the one-line budget and resource allocation structure envisaged by Jarratt, the librarian should be able to decide where cuts can be made and must shoulder the responsibility for justifying this decision to library users and staff.

Developing parallel to one-line budgets is a trend toward cost centres or budget centres. Quite a few libraries now operate under a budgeting system based on cost centres, in which overheads previously carried as a central cost by the university are devolved to individual departments and included in their budgets. Most libraries have at least some of these overheads charged to them already, especially postage and the cost of telephone calls. As far as telephones are concerned, many universities have recently installed new telephone systems which allow detailed and accurate metering of individual calls. Several libraries have had to resort to tight controls over their telephones by requiring management approval of all long-distance calls or even by discouraging all outward calls until after 1:00 p.m., when the cheaper rate is charged.

As yet, few libraries are responsible for most, or all, of their overheads. The University Library and Central Library Services of London University have had a fully devolved cost-centre budget since 1982, covering heating, lighting, telephones, rates, cloakrooms, and even parking attendants for the Senate House building. This is usually a percentage of the costs for the building which also houses other parts of the university, but when only the library is open, as on Saturdays, the full overheads are charged to the library. Other libraries with cost-centre budgets are not usually charged rates or rental for their premises, but may pay for all repairs and maintenance, as well as heating, lighting, and water, as the Bodleian does. Sussex is charged for lighting but not for heating from the central main. In future, libraries will find an increasing number of overhead costs being included in their budgets. As is already the case with telephone calls, close control will have to be kept over all aspects of cost-incurring activities. Libraries may be forced to take steps to minimize expenditure on heating and lighting; many universities have taken to keeping the heat off for as long as possible to reduce costs, and libraries may have to resort to the same tactics. From the university's point of view, this will be a welcome devolution of some difficult financial responsibilities, but from the library's point of view it may well affect at the most general level the quality of service provided to its users.

In a full-scale cost-centre budget, academic departments will also have much greater budgetary responsibilities and much greater freedom to decide how to spend their funds. This, in theory, could have a serious effect on library budgets. At several universities, there has already been talk of treating library materials as an overhead to be charged out to departments. The analogy is that the services provided by Computing Centres and Media Departments are treated as overhead, and the principle should be extended to the library. At Reading, a proposal by the Vice-Chancellor that library books should be treated as part of departmental grants was rejected by the Senate; periodicals would still have been bought from a central library fund under this scheme, but departments would have determined how much money was available for book purchases each year as part of their freedom to allocate the budget for their cost centre. Such an arrangement would destroy the library's ability to control collection development. The library is not a book-buying service for academic departments, but librarians may be forced to explain themselves and the true purpose of university libraries if cost-centre theories try to treat the library as overhead. Nevertheless, departments will have a more flexible budget, and libraries are already finding that a department may be willing to put some of this money toward the library, even when it is centrally funded. This departmental money may be for specialized services or projects, or may supplement the library's allocation for books and periodicals in a specific subject. At Reading in 1986/87, departments contributed over £13,000 to supplement a book fund which was facing a £50,000 cut. In a cost-centre budget such contributions will become less unusual, but presumably no more reliable or predictable.

The converse of this is that the library may be asked to consider charging departments for the services it provides. Several libraries already charge users for inter-library loans and many charge for on-line information retrieval. At least one makes a small charge for reservations. From the library's point of view, it would be completely undesirable to charge departments for loans, enquiries, materials, and reader places, as well as almost impossible to calculate. No reasonable university could consider taking cost-centre budgeting to such extremes. And yet this is the logical conclusion of cost centres, as long as the library is treated purely as an ancillary service. In fact, libraries are a mixture of academic department and service, taking part in the academic work of the university as well as providing services which underpin it. It follows that even in a cost-centre budget, the library should control central funds for materials and should provide its services to the academic departments while bearing the cost itself. Charges for on-line searching and inter-library loans are undesirable, though they can be justified on the grounds that each use attracts a specific charge external to the university.

One-line and cost-centre budgets are quickly becoming more common for university libraries in the wake of the Jarratt recommendations. But the place of the library in a cost-centered university is far from clear. Librarians will have to be prepared to state and justify their views on the nature of cost-centered library budgets: what they might include and what they should exclude. There are still many uncertainties to be resolved in this area over the next few years. It is worth looking more closely at one institution which is already organized into devolved cost centres, to see what may be the future budgeting arrangements for many university libraries. The library at the University of Wales Institute of Science and Technology (UWIST) is a cost centre for most overheads except rates. It receives income of three broad types: recurrent allocations from UWIST, direct grants from academic departments, and income earned from service charges. The recurrent allocation, which is over 80% of the budget, is in two parts: a percentage of the UGC recurrent grant and home student fees, and a percentage of overseas student fees. It is used for basic services, consumables, and library materials, with the restriction that overseas student funds cannot be used for long-term commitments, such as permanent staff. Grants from departmental funds are used for specialized services and staff as requested by departments (such as a Technical Reference Bureau for Architecture), for inter-library loans and on-line information retrieval, and for library materials above the basic allocation. Income is earned from photocopying, external membership fees, and so on. Apart from the departmental grants and the limits on use of funds from overseas student fees, the librarian is able to divide the budget according to the library's priorities. Departmental grants are not offset against the recurrent allocation as an excuse for reducing the allocation.

This is an example of the broad outlines of a cost-centre budget, though the exact nature of such budgets will vary considerably among different institutions. An important element is the part of the budget derived from fees paid by overseas students. Universities are all planning to increase their income from sources outside the UGC recurrent grant and home student fees, such as overseas students and research grants. Traditionally, library budgets have not been linked to these sources directly and have tended to reflect fluctuations in the university's UGC grant. But as universities reduce their dependence on that grant to the extent that as much as a third of their income may come from other sources, it is clearly in the library's interest to be assured of a reasonable share of that other income. This is especially justified by the disproportionate extra demands on library services, staff, and resources which overseas students and contract research projects make. Several libraries as well as UWIST are given a fixed percentage of overseas student fees as part of their income. Aberystwyth receives 6%, and Bangor receives 5% for art students and 3% for science students. Durham and Salford are given £100 for each overseas student. A growing number also receive a proportion of research grants. At Bath, for instance, an extra 2.5% for library materials is built into research contracts funded by sources outside the research councils. Salford has a similar 1% levy. Aberystwyth receives 6% of the overheads on research grants and Loughborough receives 5%. Academics have been unwilling in the past to consider the implications for the library of new research projects, but there are signs that this is changing. At universities like Bath the librarian can see all research proposals and comment on whether extra library materials are needed.

The same changing attitudes extend to new developments in courses and teaching. Some libraries—such as Aston, Loughborough, and Sussex—are an essential part of the procedure for approving new course proposals; without library approval and university agreement over any extra library funding needed, the course is unlikely to be accepted. This has become increasingly important at a time when the new emphasis on selectivity is resulting in the expansion of teaching and research in specific targeted subjects. The development of new self-financing courses has similar implications for libraries. In the SCONUL funding surveys, 54% of libraries reported receiving additional money from their universities for new developments in the period 1979/80 to 1984/85. In 1985/86, 34% received such funds.[2] Some of this was for buildings and automation, so the percentages were slightly lower for those receiving extra grants for new courses, "new blood" posts, and shifts in university priorities. Consideration of the library in such initiatives is therefore far from being common practice. In any case, the amounts made available are usually non-recurrent and comparatively small.

Nevertheless, the university library is more likely to have its budget linked formally in the future to changes in university priorities in teaching and research. New courses and research proposals more frequently will have an allowance for library costs built into them. As long as this is in addition to the library's budget for meeting existing needs, such a development will be a welcome acknowledgment of the library's integral part in teaching and research. It will also be necessary in a cost-centre method of budgeting, in which overheads are clearly identified and arrangements are made for meeting their cost.

While universities are turning to other sources of income, libraries do not have as much scope to do this. They already make use of various other fund sources, but none of these is a significant part of the budget. All libraries raise money from photocopying, but the first charge against this income is always the cost of providing the facilities. Quite a few libraries, usually in smaller universities, provide only the machines and consumables, but many others run a staffed photocopying service as well as self-service machines. Some, notably the copyright deposit libraries, offer a staffed service only and insist on signed requests for each copy made. Staffed services are self-financing and usually also provide the library with some surplus income, but clearly the profits are proportionally much greater with self-service copying. The amounts raised are a useful addition to a library's budget but are hardly significant. It seems likely that libraries will have to control photocopying much more closely in the future, for copyright is again becoming a major issue between universities and publishers; there may be less copying and therefore less income. Some libraries have other services like binding and photographic work, but these are self-financing rather than profit-making and require substantial investment in equipment and premises.

Other sources of income are either small and unpredictable, or larger but for a fixed period and a specific purpose. Many libraries impose fines on their borrowers for overdue books, especially from short-loan collections, but this is purely a deterrent and the amounts raised are negligible. Charges for inter-library loans and for on-line searches are intended partly to control demand and partly to offset the direct external costs incurred by the library on these services. Some libraries set their charge for inter-library loans to cover the cost of the British Library form and of communications (around £3), but others charge a purely nominal sum to discourage overuse: 30p at Newcastle and 50p at St. Andrews, for example. Most libraries charge for on-line searches, but never more than the database and communications costs. Some charge the full net cost, but many set a basic flat fee which covers searches up to a certain duration or a certain number of references retrieved. On-line searching rarely produces actual surplus income for the library.

These charges apply to internal users; for users from outside the university, full cost-recovery is usually attempted. External users are a source of income which many libraries are trying to encourage. Membership fees of £20 to £40 are often charged, but few libraries have significant numbers of external users. Those which do are mainly the large, internationally important institutions; they tend to keep their fees to a purely nominal level in recognition of these international responsibilities. Cambridge, for example, sets a maximum fee of £6 for external users. Some libraries, like the University of London Library, earn money from fees paid by American students on temporary study visits to Britain. Others play host to Open University summer schools and receive some extra funds for this. Many libraries are trying to encourage commercial firms to make use of library services, some at fees around £1,000 a year. Tenants of university science and technology parks are an obvious market for this kind of initiative, but so far on only a small scale.

External users and the fees they pay are usually, though not always, peripheral to the library's operations. It is only too likely, in any case, that funds raised in this way will be offset by the university's allocation to the library, which will be reduced accordingly. These external users will probably also require a different type and standard of service than what is given to university users, and the library is likely to find that there is a noticeable extra workload which must be met from existing staff resources. Trying to attract external users seems to offer little benefit to libraries. Such users will still come if the library has unique collections and materials. Participation in a university's promotional organization — like Salford's CAMPUS (Campaign to Promote the University of Salford) — is a better way of making the library known to the wider community.

Some libraries have generated income by selling products developed in the library. These now include computer software — Sussex sold some of its modifications to the Geac system back to Geac itself. But these sales are more likely to be items such as publications and souvenirs. Only the largest libraries have the staff and equipment to handle such materials on more than the smallest scale, and even for them the income is at best 1% or 2% of their recurrent grant. Several libraries offer surplus, unwanted, and duplicate stock for sale, sometimes to back-issue dealers and booksellers and sometimes to library users. In the latter case, this may be done through a permanent area in the library with books or journals on sale, as at Bath and Hull for example, or through a special one-day sale on a comparatively large scale, as at the University of London Library. This is a useful way of turning unwanted stock into an asset, though the amounts raised are likely insignificant. A cautious approach is vital to public book sales since they can easily upset academics and donors who would rather see the material retained by the library. The university may also insist on deducting sale income from the library's allocation.

Universities are pursuing an active policy of fund-raising, especially with commercial firms and philanthropic foundations. Libraries are sometimes part of this trend and are among the specific areas of university activity suggested to potential donors. At Exeter, the new library building was funded in part by a £750,000 gift from Dubai, and the library continues to appear prominently in the university's promotional booklet. Oxford University's Development Officer, appointed with considerable publicity in 1986, has included the Bodleian and his fund-raising activities. But in general, libraries have had little benefit from university fund-raising so far and it seems unlikely that this will change much in the near future, despite the speed with which universities are abandoning their previous attitudes and rushing to advertise and promote themselves.

Fund-raising by the library itself appears no more promising. The success of Cambridge's Department of Oriental and Other Languages in raising funds depends heavily on the unique nature of its Genizah manuscript collection, its interest to particular ethnic groups, and the amount of conservation, cataloguing, and research needed to bring out the full value of the collection. Where such fund-raising is possible, it is inevitably linked to highly specialized areas or to specific projects which require capital, such as automation. It is not a realistic option for increasing a library's recurrent budget.

A more promising area of university activity is the increasing frequency of fund-raising from former students, usually given the American name "alumni associations." At Nottingham, a Graduates Library Fund organized by the University's Convocation makes an annual contribution of several thousand pounds to the library's budget. Glasgow has also received donations from graduands. This is a field in which libraries are beginning to show more interest; some offer special membership rights to graduates. The larger libraries, and some of the smaller ones, have established Friends of the Library, which include as one of their main purposes fund-raising for the library. The money is usually for purchasing materials which are expensive and otherwise unobtainable, but at Brunel the Friends mainly intend to supplement general book funds.

The larger libraries have a fairly substantial income from bequests, endowments, and trust funds. Some smaller libraries also receive this sort of income, though on a fairly small scale: St Andrews, for example, has a new endowment fund which earns interest equivalent to about 4% of the library's non-staff grant, while Reading has a comparatively small income from endowments associated with its special collections. But funds like these, whatever their size, are almost always earmarked for purchasing specific types of library materials, and can rarely be used to supplement general funds. Also earmarked are funds from government bodies, which are either for specific projects or for providing services to non-university users. Grants from the British Library are for research, conservation, and similar projects, while grants are made by the National Health Service for medical libraries open to Health Service users. Funds from the Manpower Services Commission have frequently been used, chiefly for retrospective conversion projects. Fifteen libraries reported using Commission funds in the period 1979/80-1984/85 and a further 11 in SCONUL's survey for 1985/86.

In 1987, earmarked funds were also made available for libraries by the UGC, which had previously avoided direct provision as much as possible. A total of £3 million for each of the years 1987/88 to 1989/90 was assigned for the purchase of books and periodicals, divided (at least for the first year) in proportion to each university's student numbers. This was regarded by libraries as something of a mixed blessing, since the funds were for three years only, and would mean a greater workload at a time of falling staff numbers. Most importantly, the universities were not obliged to treat this as extra to the recurrent allocation for their libraries. At universities like Hull and Sussex, it seemed likely that the extra UGC grant would be used merely to soften the severity of planned reductions in library budgets. The UGC also set aside between £1.5 million and £2 million to be used in providing communications equipment for linking library computer systems to campus networks and to the Joint Academic Network (JANET).

The UGC has been reluctant to consider making direct provision for university libraries, on the grounds that this would "pre-empt university decisions and remove responsibility and accountability from the management of universities"; in its view, a university "should determine the internal disposition of its grant in accordance with its own plans and priorities."[3] It has agreed to establish a sub-committee to advise it on matters relating to libraries, but has not had the financial resources to do so. Among the proposals for earmarked grants which this sub-committee would consider are: retrospective conversion, capital funding for automation, and funds for collections with special significance outside the university. But until the transition to the new Universities Funding Council is complete, the future of earmarked grants from this source is unclear.

The importance of external funds should not be overestimated. In SCONUL surveys of funding, 49% of the libraries which replied said they had received earmarked external funds in the period 1979/80 to 1984/85; 26% had received some non-earmarked external funds. For 1985/86, 28% had received earmarked funds and 13% had received non-earmarked funds. When such funds are forthcoming, they are much more likely to be for a specific purpose, usually with a limited duration. Like so many of a library's potential sources of income, they have very little relevance to the main recurrent budget.

Libraries will remain dependent on the university for virtually all of that budget, despite an increasing interest in other ways of raising funds. And, since universities are being required to account to the government for their use of public money, libraries will find this demand for accountability passed on to them. But no standard performance measures for university libraries have yet been developed, despite considerable investigation of various lines of research. The emphasis for performance measures of universities is being placed on unit costs and ratios, and comparative assessment of inputs and outputs (basically new students and qualified graduates, respectively). The CVCP and the government are expecting similar measures to be developed for university libraries. Comparative ratios for many aspects of library operations were produced in a pilot study by the Centre for Interfirm Comparisons in 1984, covering 12 libraries of varying sizes.[4] Unit costs were calculated for items such as each volume acquired, each loan transaction, and each inter-library loan. Ratios were given under headings such as expenditure per head of permanent user population, database searches per head of user population, and short loans per head of student population.

SCONUL has developed its own statistical database which enables the calculation of comparative ratios relating to library finance and operations. The first part of this database gives percentages for different types of expenditure within the library's budget, and for library expenditure within the university budget; it also gives the amount of expenditure in various categories per student (full-time equivalent) and per library staff member. The second part gives percentages for different types of use of shelving, average seats occupied, outgoing inter-library loans against incoming ones, and the inter-library loan success rate. It produces ratios measured as the rate per 100 potential university users for amount of shelving, level of acquisitions, seating, users present, enquiries, loans, and overall service activity. There are also rates per 100 loans for consultations, reservations, and recalls or overdues. The results are analysed by grouping together libraries in universities of similar type: Oxbridge, London, Larger Civic, Smaller Civic, Ancient Scottish, Welsh, Technological, and New. Libraries are also grouped according to the number of students in each university. A few libraries do not provide statistics or insist that their figures are kept confidential.[5]

SCONUL regards its expenditure statistics as more accurate and useful than the less detailed tables published as part of the UGC University Statistical Record's *University statistics, part 3, Finance*. It hopes to have its statistical database recognized by the UGC and CVCP as the authoritative source of university library statistics, and would prefer performance measures to be based on SCONUL data instead of the University Statistical Record's data. But in their present form neither set of statistics should be used as measures of performance. Comparisons of library costs per full-time-equivalent student, or of library expenditure as a percentage of university expenditure, can easily be made and have been frequently used, in a highly selective and partial way, by librarians and university administrators alike. Unless SCONUL can develop its own performance measures these crude and misleading comparisons are likely to be treated as performance measures by default.

SCONUL is now working toward its own measures, as an alternative to the CVCP's proposal for "cost per full-time-equivalent student." The measure which SCONUL is considering will be expressed in terms of "hours of use per £." The elements involved are library expenditure, a measure of use in the library, and circulation statistics. The last of these will be used in conjunction with a ratio between the length of time for which an item is kept on loan and the number of hours of eye-contact with the item by the user during that time. This ratio relies on the research done on "document exposure time" in the early 1970s. The performance measure will therefore be based on the relationship between expenditure on a library and an estimate of the amount of time its users spend actually looking at the library's materials.

None of the suggested ratios, however, makes allowances for variations caused by the unique circumstances of each library: its buildings, subject coverage, emphasis on particular services, and so on. SCONUL is compiling profiles of all libraries to take note of these circumstances, but these factors would have to be included as a measurable element of statistical analyses if a realistic comparison of ratios is to be made. Otherwise, these ratios are quite misleading without lengthy footnotes giving accounts of exceptional circumstances. This is especially important since all these measures are purely comparative; there has been no attempt to set minimum acceptable levels for library expenditure and operations.

The government's aim in insisting on performance measures is to ensure that the universities are providing value for money. All the measures which are likely to be applied to libraries define "value" in purely quantitative terms. A library is assumed to be giving greater value if it provides more loans more cheaply per student, or if more enquiries are handled by staff who are paid at a lower than average cost. University libraries have always preferred to consider their own value in qualitative terms: the quality of the help given to users, the contribution of library services and collections to the quality of research and undergraduate work, and so on. These are, by any reasonable assessment, unmeasurable in the statistical sense. At a more specific level, it is possible to measure how successful libraries are in providing users with access to information and materials: how often users find what they are looking for in the catalogue or on the shelf, how long it takes them to find specific materials or information, the extent to which on-line searches provide relevant references. But such measures are not a realistic option, since they require substantial extra staff or sophisticated automated systems to compile the data, and standard research methodologies are not available.

Since performance measures appear to be inevitable, libraries will have to choose between having crude quantitative measures imposed on them and developing only slightly less crude measures themselves. SCONUL, like the universities, has pragmatically chosen the latter path. It remains to be seen what purposes these performance measures will be used for, and what effect a comparatively poor result will have on a library's funding.

Performance measures and all these changes in governance and funding must be seen in the context of severe constraints on funding. Almost all libraries have had a difficult time financially since the government cut university grants so drastically in 1981. The universities estimate that their income fell by 17% in real terms between 1979/80 and 1984/85, and for most this fall is set to continue.[6] Most universities claim to have tried to protect their libraries from the full effects of this decline in income — at least in the sense of cutting the library budget at a rate less than that of departmental allocations, as at Exeter and Surrey, or by holding library funds level while reducing departmental budgets, as at Birmingham in 1986/87. But, despite this claim, the overall statistics tell a different story. The library share of total university recurrent expenditure in British universities fell by 9.6% between 1979/80 and 1984/85, as Table 2.1 shows.[7]

Table 2.1 Library share of university recurrent expenditure (Great Britain)

	University Recurrent Expenditure £000	Library Recurrent Expenditure £000	Library Share
1979/80	1,257,122	52,127	4.15%
1980/81	1,555,551	62,717	4.03%
1981/82	1,686,629	64,574	3.83%
1982/83	1,847,021	69,175	3.74%
1983/84	1,975,957	74,855	3.79%
1984/85	2,139,721	80,259	3.75%

This trend has continued in subsequent years. At Stirling, library expenditure rose 18% between 1980/81 and 1985/86, while academic expenditure rose 34% (excluding research contracts), or 64% if research contracts are included. The libraries at Hull and Sussex are now having their share of university expenditure deliberately reduced, on the grounds that they were overfunded in the past. The special UGC allocation for library materials during the period 1987/88 to 1989/90 may halt this decline in the libraries' share of university expenditure, but much depends on whether the universities are willing to treat it as an addition to the library budget, rather than as a way of reducing expenditure on the library from university recurrent funds.

With this declining share of a declining budget, libraries have had to cope with a continuing high rate of inflation for library materials. The Index of University Costs calculated a rise of almost 70% between 1981 and 1985 in the cost of books, periodicals, and binding.[8] This is very much a minimum estimate of the rate of inflation, for reasons which are discussed in Chapter 4. But even using this Index as a measure, the decline in real expenditure is dramatic:

Table 2.2 Expenditure in real terms on library materials (Great Britain)

	Cash expenditure £M	% of 1980/81 expenditure in real terms	Expenditure at 1980/81 prices £M
1980/81	23.0	100	23.0
1981/82	23.6	87	20.0
1982/83	26.4	86	19.8
1983/84	29.5	82	18.9
1984/85	31.1	79	18.2

When the rate of inflation on library materials (as measured by the Index of University Costs) is taken into account, libraries had 21% less to spend on materials in 1984/85 than in 1980/81. The National Book League, using the Retail Price Index as its measure instead, calculated a fall in real expenditure of 18% between 1980/81 and 1983/84.[9] This decline has not been reversed since then, and the uncertainty about the UGC's earmarked grant affects predictions for the next few years.

This rapid deterioration in the general financial position of university libraries has affected all their activities. In the SCONUL survey of cuts between 1979/80 and 1984/85, 77% of libraries said they had cut the number of monographs they bought, mostly by more than 20%. periodicals had been cut by 75% of libraries. The academic-related staff was reduced by 79%, and 75% had reduced their clerical staff, usually by 10 to 15%. Opening hours had been cut in 55% of libraries. SCONUL's next survey was of cuts in 1985/86 alone, but in that year 38% of libraries had further reduced their purchases of monographs and 32% had cut more periodical subscriptions. Further reductions in academic-related staff were reported by 25%; 30% had cut clerical staff. Reductions in all these areas have continued since then.

These overall figures conceal considerable local variations. Some libraries were heavily cut in 1981/82, but are now improving their position rapidly. Others have declined gradually and are now facing an uncertain future. Others are making more serious cuts now than at any time in the past six years. Still others, mainly the largest libraries, have only recently come under strong financial pressure. These variations mirror the varying fortunes of their parent institutions and are likely to increase in extent under the new UGC policy of more selective funding. Despite this variation, it is undoubtedly true that all British university libraries have had to make cuts since 1981 in at least one major area of their activities, whether services, staffing, or materials. Most libraries have had to cut activities in all areas, often to a substantial degree.

REFERENCES

1. Veaner, Allen B. "1985 to 1995: The next decade in academic librarianship" *College and research libraries* 46 (1985), pp. 209-229, 295-308.
2. SCONUL. *Survey of funding cuts 1979/80-1984/85* (Doc. 86/27); *Survey of funding 1984/85-1985/86* (Doc. 87/48).
3. Library Association. University, College and Research Section. *U C & R newsletter* 20 (Nov. 1986), pp. 10-11.
4. Centre for Interfirm Comparisons. *Inter-library comparisons in academic libraries*. BL R&D reports, no. 5763 (1984).
5. SCONUL. *University library expenditure statistics*, 1981/82– ; *SCONUL statistical database part II, library operations*, 1984/85–
6. SCONUL. *Annual report* 1986, p. 94.
7. Tables 2.1 & 2.2 are based on tables in SCONUL *Annual report* 1986, p. 94, 98, updated for 1984/85 from *University Statistics, vol. 3, Finance*.
8. SCONUL. *Annual report* 1986, p. 96.
9. National Book League. *Library book and periodical spending in universities, polytechnics and colleges, 1981-84* (London: National Book League, 1986).

Chapter 3

Staffing

Substantial staff cuts have been a continual necessity in British university libraries. All the non-specialized libraries have had to make reductions in staff since 1979/80. The SCONUL survey of funding cuts, which includes some smaller, specialized libraries, found that 79% of libraries had reduced their number of academic-related posts between 1979/80 and 1984/85, most commonly by 14 to 29%. Reductions in the number of clerical posts had been made by 75% of libraries, most commonly by 9 to 16%. Other posts, such as bindery and photographic staff, porters and cleaners, had been reduced in 45% of the libraries which had this type of post, most commonly by 14 to 29%. In some cases, the number of clerical and academic-related posts had been cut by one-third. Further cuts were reported for 1985/86, with another 25% of libraries reducing academic-related posts and 30% reducing clerical posts. There have been further reductions since then, and more are planned.

By any standards, these figures represent a substantial and rapid decline in library staffing. For many libraries, their staffing is now "on a knife-edge," as several librarians described it. Service points for general and specialized services are having to restrict their operating hours; notices saying that services are unavailable because of staff shortages are an increasingly common sight. Many libraries find it difficult or impossible to cover for illness, holidays, or other reasons for staff being absent. Libraries with several sites are endeavouring to rationalize and reduce staff at these sites. Aberdeen withdrew most of the staff from its old King's College Library in 1983, to help in staff reductions. Edinburgh has pursued a policy of rationalizing its many sites, partly at least to reduce staff, but has also been forced to stop staffing its enquiry desk in the foyer of the main library building. Further staff cuts at Bangor would probably mean the closure of one of its five sites.

Many libraries have been given targets for staff reductions. In some cases, the university or the Library Committee has specified a percentage of staffing expenditures to be saved. Southampton cut staff by 11% in 1981-1984; this was the rate at which the university's total income was cut. The Bodleian has been asked to make an 11% cut between 1986 and 1991, while Bradford has been told to cut its staff by 5% by 1991. Other libraries have had this target expressed as a percentage of their total budget. Newcastle has the power to set its own staffing levels to a maximum of 47% of its budget. Sheffield is aiming to reduce its expenditure on staff from 47% to 45% by 1990, having already reduced it from 55% in 1981. These targets can also be given in cash terms; Edinburgh had £23,500 cut from its staff budget in 1985/86, and Leicester £30,000 in the same year. A university Working Party on Library Staffing at Stirling reduced the staffing target there by £10,000. Sheffield was given a target reduction of £45,000 on staff for 1986-1988, while Aberdeen had its 1986/87 budget cut by £12,000.

A separate staff budget renders a library particularly vulnerable to these kinds of target reductions. Even with a one-line budget, librarians do not always have a free hand in determining their own level of staffing. The university may set a maximum percentage of this budget which can be allocated to staff, as at Newcastle, or may direct the library to reduce staff as part of a university-wide staffing review. But a one-line budget usually gives the librarian greater flexibility in deciding where cuts will be made, if they are required by the university. In at least two London colleges which have one-line budgets, the librarian has followed a policy of cutting staff quite sharply, in order to protect the budget for books and periodicals. For most libraries, though, the decision as to where cuts will fall has usually been made by the university or the Library Committee, often ignoring the advice of the librarian. At Bristol, the Library Committee went against the librarian's advice and decided that the 1981 cuts should fall mainly on staff. Such decisions on staffing cuts used to be made hurriedly, in an atmosphere of crisis; now they are more likely to be the outcome of university plans.

In those libraries with separate staffing budgets, the university also exercises its control every time there is a vacancy. Many libraries are in the position of having to obtain university approval before filling any vacant position paid for from central recurrent funds. The university usually builds in substantial delay between when the vacancy occurs and when the new occupant takes up the post, if approval to fill is given. It took more than six months to fill the Deputy's position at Reading, and this is far from unusual. Chief librarians' posts have sometimes remained vacant for long periods, partly at least for the university to save money; the position of librarian at Aberdeen was vacant for over 18 months from 1986. These substantial delays affect all levels of post, clerical as well as academic-related, and aggravate considerably the difficulties and frustrations caused by the many posts which are not filled at all. A few libraries, like Birmingham and Cambridge, have been able to reach agreement with their university on a new staffing establishment for clerical staff; Hull is also aiming for such an agreement. This at least enables the library to make its own decisions about filling clerical vacancies, and avoids the necessity of having to obtain university approval before filling every vacant post for a library assistant.

Reading is unusual in having reached agreement on a new establishment for the whole of its staff, after large-scale cuts in senior posts. This means that university approval is not needed before a vacancy is filled, but it does not avoid a substantial delay in filling vacancies which result from the university's appointment procedures. Nor does it rule out the possibility of having some of these posts frozen in the future under a university staffing plan. Quite a few libraries still have, in theory, a staffing establishment which is rather larger than their existing staff numbers and contains various frozen, unfilled posts. Freezing vacant posts is the usual reaction to a sudden need to reduce expenditure on staffing; one of the measures taken when the seriousness of Cardiff's financial problems become clear was to freeze all vacant posts. Freezing a post means postponing a decision on whether that post will be filled or abolished, though in the prevailing financial climate most frozen posts are likely to be abolished eventually. In this sense they do not offer libraries much cause for optimism.

Reduction of expenditure on staffing remains a major goal of all universities, making it much more probable that frozen vacancies will not be filled. Even when vacancies are allowed to be filled, libraries have often been put under pressure to fill them at a lower level. This "trading down" has been applied to senior academic-related posts in various libraries, and particularly to the position of deputy librarian. Bristol replaced one of its two deputies with a senior library assistant, while Hull and Newcastle replaced their deputy with a sub-librarian. Bradford replaced two sub-librarians with assistant librarians. St Andrews has pursued a policy of replacing one senior post with two junior posts. Filling vacancies at a lower level has been resorted to by universities all over Britain as another means of reducing expenditure on staff, while at least giving libraries a replacement member of staff.

All these measures — abolishing posts, freezing posts, and filling posts at a lower level — have been used to enable universities to cut the staffing budget of their libraries. The result is that total spending on staff, which had risen by 2% in 1980/81, rose at an average of only 5% a year between 1981/82 and 1984/85.[1]

Table 3.1 Library recurrent expenditure on staff (Great Britain)

	Total staff expenditure (£000)	Index (1980/81 = 100)
1979/80	28,496	79
1980/81	36,267	100
1981/82	37,032	102
1982/83	38,450	106
1983/84	40,979	113
1984/85	43,729	121

The brake on staff expenditure is most obvious in the immediate aftermath of the 1981 cuts, when the total amount spent in Great Britain remained almost static. Staffing costs rose by 22% for academic-related staff and 33% for other staff between 1980/81 and 1984/85, according to the Index of University Costs. Library staff expenditure therefore fell in real terms during this period. At the same time, the share of libraries' recurrent expenditure for staff was falling, from 58% to 54% according to the UGC's figures.

These general statistics conceal considerable variations in different types of libraries. SCONUL's measure of library staff expenditure per student (full-time-equivalent) rose 18.2% between 1981/82 and 1984/85 (compared with a rise of 37.6% in acquisitions expenditure per student). But in the technological universities the median increase in staff expenditure per student was only 8.8%, and in the Welsh colleges it was 9.6%.[2] Similarly, staff recurrent expenditure in the technological universities rose only 13% between 1980/81 and 1984/85, compared with the average of 21%. The rise was 34% for Cambridge and Oxford in the same period, according to the UGC statistics.

Despite all the staff reductions, expenditure has gradually accelerated since 1982. In part this may be due to filling some previously frozen posts, but the major causes have been salary rises and "incremental drift." The latter results from a greater proportion of staff than before reaching the top of the salary scale for their grade, since staff mobility at the academic-related level has been very low. The effect of salary rises on staff expenditure has been accelerated even further with the agreement between the universities, the government, and the Association of University Teachers (AUT) in early 1987 for an overall rise of 24% in academic-related salaries. Of this, 16.6% was payable in 1 December 1986, and the remainder in March 1988. This rise immediately caused difficulties for library staffing budgets, and there will undoubtedly be further pressure to reduce academic-related staff in the next few years.

The 24% rise included as one of the AUT's concessions a complete re-grading of the academic-related staff in libraries. Since 1974, a national grading scheme had linked library staff to academic staff grades; in its simplest form, this meant that Assistant Librarian, Sub-Librarian, and Librarian were equivalent to Lecturer, Senior Lecturer, and Professor. The application of this varied between universities. For some, assistant librarians were on the full lecturer scale, with automatic increments to the top; other libraries split this scale in two, with a bar to prevent automatic progression from the lower half of the upper. Promotion on merit or length of service, rather than responsibility, was possible even to the level of sub-librarian. The 1987 salary grades reduced the link to academic scales to little more than a "salary spine" of the same salary points. Academic-related staff will now be on six grades, only two of which (sub-librarian and librarian) are the same as academic grades. Promotion from grade one to grade two will depend on satisfactory performance and a demonstrated ability to undertake a higher level of duties. Promotion from grade two to grade three will usually be linked to a definite increase in duties, though promotion on merit is not entirely ruled out. Promotion beyond this will be only on the basis of an increase in duties and responsibilities. There is also provision for accelerated increments within a grade to reward outstanding staff, as well as extra discretionary points at the top of grade five, and a grade four which overlaps grades three and five.

Libraries are having to re-grade their existing academic-related staff with this different structure, though its relationship to existing hierarchies is far from clear. Some assistant librarians previously on the long lecturers' scale will now be on grade three, though their duties do not differ much from those of assistant librarians now on grade two and previously on the lower half of a two-stage lecturer scale. New assistant librarians, who will not normally go beyond grade two without greater responsibilities, are likely to resent older colleagues on grade three without such responsibilities. All academic-related posts, as distinct from their present occupants, will have to be graded under the new structure. For many libraries, this will cause considerable difficulties, since there is usually no intermediate post in the library hierarchy between assistant librarian and sub-librarian. It is clear that there will have to be a more complex hierarchical structure for academic-related staff in future. This will only serve to weaken further the idea of a link with academic staff and their essentially collegial rather than hierarchical organization.

Another effect of this re-grading will be to make job descriptions more necessary. Few academic-related staff at present hold posts with a detailed job description attached. Like academics, they are appointed to a grade rather than a post and can, in theory, be expected to undertake any tasks of a suitable level. This flexibility is greatest in smaller libraries like Surrey, where academic-related staff are responsible for several different tasks at once and where organizational structures can be fairly fluid. Under the new salary scales, the duties of each academic-related position will need to be identified and specified in order to justify its grading. Libraries may lose much of the flexibility they have had in assigning tasks to academic-related staff and in transferring such staff to different responsibilities. Internal movement of academic-related staff on a large scale, as has happened recently at Newcastle and Sussex, will be much more difficult when the natural inertia of many individuals is reinforced by a more closely defined system of grading posts according to their responsibilities.

The new academic-related grades are also tied to regular appraisal and assessment of staff. The universities have not yet been able to agree on the methods of carrying out such appraisal, but they are under considerable pressure from the government to introduce it. Very few libraries undertake any formal assessment of academic-related staff at present, though some assess their staff by informal means. Sussex is unusual in having an annual interview and report to the vice-chancellor on all its academic-related staff. In the future, appraisal of library staff may be based on local or national criteria, but these will differ from those used for academic staff and will further emphasize the gap between academic and academic-related staff. Appraisal will certainly demand considerable extra time, training, and record-keeping, but additional funds to allow for this seem unlikely. At present, it looks as if appraisal for academic-related staff will be largely negative, since there will be few means of rewarding outstanding performance or of furthering the career of most staff.

Academic-related staff are now a much smaller group than in the past. Their numbers fell from 1,490 in 1980/81 to 1,331 in 1984/85, a reduction of 11%.[3] Even allowing for early retirements and vacancies caused by promotion, this has meant that there has been only a very slow trickle of new recruits to academic-related positions. It is now almost impossible for a suitably qualified graduate to get an academic-related position as their first post. The only exception might be for a person with very specialized qualifications being recruited for an equally specialized post. New professionals must usually start their careers as senior library assistants, or a similar high clerical grade, and wait for an opportunity to apply for promotion to an academic-related post. Such promotions are fairly rare and are often made internally. The effect has been to blur the connection between professional qualifications and the post held, and to create a sizeable group of often frustrated and disgruntled staff who are qualified to hold an academic-related post but who have next to no chance of obtaining it. Many libraries have followed a policy of taking overqualified people for clerical positions and they are now faced with the consequences, which do nothing to help general morale.

Senior library assistants and chief library assistants are now often doing work previously done by academic-related staff. This is especially true in cataloguing, which has been transferred to senior clerical positions partly as a result of greater automation and use of outside bibliographic records, but also to reduce costs and redeploy academic-related staff to reader service duties. Senior clerical staff are likely to hold posts with administrative responsibilities, such as head of the issue desk or head of inter-library loans, unlike most academic-related subject specialists who have no such duties. It is hardly surprising, then, that senior library assistants who are graduate professionals often feel that the library is exploiting them. Several libraries are trying to reduce these problems by limiting their senior clerical grades to junior graduate professionals, but this can only be done slowly since the staff currently in these grades are usually permanent and include people with no qualifications who have been promoted on ability alone, as well as people with either professional qualifications or a degree but not both. If the senior library assistant grade can be made exclusively for junior graduate professionals eligible for promotion to academic-related posts, the frustrations and tensions evident at present will be reduced, though not abolished.

Frustrations also affect academic-related staff, mainly concerning a remarkable lack of mobility. Almost all libraries still have the same people in academic-related posts as they had when the cuts began in 1981. There are occasional exceptions, notably Aston, where turnover of academic-related staff has been at a high level. But for most libraries the only movement has been when staff take early retirement or (in the case of the large libraries like Manchester and Cambridge) are promoted to higher posts elsewhere. The almost universal picture is of the same group of people, doing much the same duties, with the occasional internal promotion, while the overall size of the group gradually shrinks. This is not a recipe for high morale, and many libraries now have considerable difficulty motivating this group and keeping them interested in their work.

In complete contrast, there has been a dramatic turnover in chief librarians since the 1981 cuts. Roughly half the university libraries have had a new chief librarian since 1981; in some the turnover has been even more rapid—Surrey has had three chief librarians in quick succession. An additional three libraries changed librarian in late 1987 (Birmingham, Reading, and Sussex), while Aberdeen had to wait over 18 months in 1986-88. This turnover has not had a major flow-on effect, since many of the positions which the new librarians had held (notably that of deputy) were abolished or downgraded after their promotion. There is a marked contrast between many new chief librarians, eager to bring new ideas to their libraries, and their academic-related staff, who have had little opportunity to move to new jobs, and this has often added to problems of morale and motivation.

Turnover has been much greater at the clerical level in most libraries, since clerical posts are less likely to be filled by people looking for a permanent career. Nevertheless, some libraries have experienced comparatively little movement even of clerical staff, and many senior library assistants have held their posts for many years regardless of their qualifications. Most, but not all, libraries use national salary scales for clerical positions, and job descriptions are more common for clerical staff. But these scales offer only a fairly limited career structure, quite separate from that for academic-related staff and with much lower employers' costs. As a result, clerical staff are mainly either young people in their late teens and early 20s or older, married women returning to work after raising a family. Most clerical staff are women, whereas over half the academic-related staff, and most of the staff above assistant librarian, are men.[4] The tensions inherent in this pattern of staffing have increased in recent years with the shrinking numbers of academic-related staff, the increasing proportion of graduate professionals among the clerical staff, and the "trading down" of academic-related posts to clerical posts.

There are also new trends emerging which affect clerical staff rather more than academic-related staff. A growing number of libraries are appointing new staff on temporary contracts; some of these apply to all levels of staff, others are only for appointments below the level of senior library assistant. The normal pattern for most staff, however, remains a permanent appointment after a period of probation, which can only be terminated "for good cause" (or perhaps because of redundancy due to financial difficulties, which some universities are now including in new conditions of appointment). At a time when flexibility in staffing is essential, there will be increasing pressure from universities for the use of temporary contracts in libraries. At Buckingham, where all staff are given three-year contracts, the university is obliged to give one year's notice if the contract is not to be renewed. But many university libraries are tied to an unnecessarily high proportion of permanent appointments and greater flexibility would be desirable. However, too many temporary contracts will create a climate of uncertainty and weaken the depth of long-term contribution which staff can make. There needs to be a balance between permanent and temporary which protects the interests of the library and individual staff. Above all, universities must avoid drawing a further dividing line between academic staff and library staff over the question of length of appointment, and libraries must avoid a similar division between academic-related staff and other staff.

Another trend is for libraries to employ more part-time staff. Again, this is more noticeable among clerical staff, though the number of part-time, academic-related staff rose 65% between 1981 and 1985 according to UGC statistics.[5] The total number remains small in comparison to full-time, academic-related positions, however. Part-time clerical staff have become much more common, and several libraries employ them on a large scale. At Sussex, 34 out of 55 clerical staff were part-time in 1987, while at Kent 35 clerical positions were shared among about 85 staff. These part-time clerical staff are often employed in specialized ways. Quite a few libraries use such staff only for evening and weekend duties at issue desks. Others have a pool of part-time staff purely to do the shelving. A growing number of libraries employ part-time clerical staff for loans work during term-time only. These part-time appointments are mainly intended to overcome the problem of keeping loans services available at the same level despite overall staff reductions. Other approaches to this problem involve rostering all clerical staff, including those in technical services departments, to work on issue desks, or opening the library at weekends and in the evenings without services. Special part-time staff for these tasks allow the library to direct its limited manpower to meet specific demands. But the cost is a much more fragmented staff, with less sense of teamwork and increased difficulties in control and communication. Nevertheless, this is a measure which more libraries are likely to be forced to adopt in the future.

More libraries also pay for some staff from funds other than their recurrent grant. Some sections of a library are partly or wholly self-financing from earned income, and photocopying, photographic, and binding staff have traditionally been funded in this way. Newer ventures, like Warwick's Business Information Service, also earn money toward staff costs, while at UWIST (University of Wales Institute of Science and Technology) departments requiring special services contribute to relevant staff costs from their departmental budgets. There are also grants from outside bodies, such as the British Library and the Manpower Services Commission, for special conservation, cataloguing, and research projects. But these funds from outside sources have almost always been used for staff who are peripheral to the library's main activities, working on tasks and services which are either limited in time or in clientele.

In general, then, staff levels are barely adequate to carry on the traditional activities of university libraries. In some cases, they are less than adequate. Libraries are turning to more part-time staff, more contract staff, and other sources of funding to try and maintain the quality of their services. At the same time, they are often having to reorganize the structure of staffing and management. The cuts in staff numbers, especially those at the academic-related level, have made it impossible for many libraries to carry on with the same organizational structure which they had before 1981. Other factors, especially increasing automation, growing financial difficulties and complexities, and the increasing number of graduate professional staff in clerical posts, are also pushing toward necessary restructuring. To achieve the best management control over a rapidly changing situation and to provide the best deployment of shrinking staff resources, libraries are having to alter their organizational structure. But a strong brake on this change is the very low turnover of academic-related staff, some of whom are resistant or indifferent to change.

One of the most frequent signs of organizational change has been the position of deputy librarians. Before the 1981 cuts, most libraries (except the smallest) had a deputy, whose main duties were usually to oversee staffing (especially non-academic-related) and to take charge of routine administration and day-to-day problems, while the librarian dealt with planning, finance, and relations with the university. Reporting through the deputy to the librarian were all the departments and divisions of the library. Since 1981, so many libraries have lost the deputy's position that a deputy librarian is now unusual in all but the largest libraries. In exchange, permission has often been given to promote an assistant librarian to an extra sub-librarian's position. Most libraries have been left with a group of sub-librarians directly responsible to the librarian. This has resulted in the creation of what are in effect management teams, usually consisting of the librarian and from two to five sub-librarians, who meet regularly and frequently to consider management issues relating to routine activities and forward planning. The duty of deputizing in the librarian's absence is often rotated among the sub-librarians.

This change has, in fact, had its benefits. These management teams offer a more coordinated and broadly based approach to management at a time of increasing difficulties and complexities. They enable a better balance between outward-looking and inward-looking responsibilities, since the librarian is more involved in day-to-day decisions and the sub-librarians are more involved in issues relating to the university's planning and budgeting, now that these outside issues are more pressing and time-consuming than ever before. Whether management teams make decisions or simply advise the librarian depends on the individuals involved, but they do provide a route for decision making which is potentially more flexible and which shares the burden of management. A few libraries have developed this kind of management team even with a deputy; at Southampton, the deputy and the three sub-librarians in charge of divisions all report directly to the librarian and function as a team, with the deputy responsible for the User Services division. It is clear that for many libraries (except perhaps the largest) this type of structure meets changing managerial needs better than the deputy's position could.

The number of different divisions and sub-units reporting to the librarian (sometimes through a deputy) and the duties which each carries out vary greatly. This is partly a consequence of library size; a library with a large staff carrying out many tasks is bound to have a more complex and specialized organizational structure, while a smaller library can be simpler and more flexible. Another major factor is the number of sites on which the library is housed; a library like Edinburgh or Bristol, with many subsidiary sites outside the main building, requires a different type of organization from single-site libraries like Aston or Sussex. A third important influence is the history of the library itself; long-established staff structures are difficult to change, especially at a time when turnover of senior staff is very low and inertia is correspondingly high. All these factors encourage local variations to the extent that there is no standard pattern of organization in British university libraries, even among those of similar size and age. But there are themes and trends in staffing which apply generally and which are important considerations at a time when all libraries are having to re-examine their staffing.

An underlying theme is the degree to which the organizational structure is diffuse or concentrated. At one extreme is a simple division into technical services and user services like that at Reading, with the latter covering subject librarians, special collections, and branch libraries, and the former covering cataloguing, book orders, periodicals, and binding. Lending services would normally come under user services, though at Reading they are assigned to the technical services division to distinguish them from reference and information services. The heads of the two divisions report directly to the librarian.

Aston divides its staff into Library Services (covering acquisitions, bibliographic records, and all aspects of document supply), and Information and User Education Services. Some libraries, such as Birmingham and Edinburgh, are at the other extreme, with eight or nine units of varying sizes reporting to the librarian (either directly or through a deputy). Most libraries are in the middle of these two extremes, often with four or five divisions reporting to the librarian. But clearly the more diffuse the spread of responsibility, the more complex management becomes; control and coordination are harder to maintain. Libraries with several sites have special difficulties and much depends on the size, location, and subject coverage of branch libraries if they are to be integrated into the staff structure rather than treated as a disparate group. The normal pattern is for branch libraries to be responsible individually or in groups to the librarian or deputy. It is rarely possible for them to be represented directly on a senior management team or to have a broad range of tasks devolved to them.

Another question closely related to diffused control concerns the extent to which a hierarchical structure exists in reality as well as on paper. Some libraries, like Bradford and Kent, have a fluid form of organization where reporting lines and hierarchies are left unclear. Most libraries with subject specialists are likely to experience this kind of fluid structure, though it may be limited to reference and information services rather than operate as a general principle. The usual pattern is for a considerable degree of hierarchy to exist for library divisions other than subject librarians: a unit responsible for carrying out a particular function, such as serials control or interlibrary loans, is subsumed under the more general control of an acquisitions or technical services librarian or a reader services librarian. In some cases, these hierarchies may be theoretical rather than working in practice. Cambridge has a hierarchy of divisions which are each composed of several departments, but the divisions are neither concrete nor under the control of an overall divisional head since one of the department heads doubles as divisional head. In most libraries hierarchical structures are valuable and necessary, as long as they are not applied too rigidly. Rigid hierarchies among academic-related staff reduce further their similarity to academic staff, who have a basically collegial organization; they also lead to a loss of flexibility and an inability to respond quickly to changing circumstances. Conversely, a staff structure which is too loose makes it hard for the chief librarian to manage the library effectively, as described in the Jarratt recommendations.

Most libraries now have a hybrid structure which mixes the functional division and the subject-based approach. Some still have a basically functional organization, while a few — like the Bodleian — retain a division by types of material, at least in theory. In those libraries with some form of organization of staff by subjects, the scope and nature of subject responsibilities vary considerably. In most, this subject coverage is limited to certain members of the academic-related staff, who have no other duties. A few libraries extend responsibility for detailed enquiries and collection development in specific subjects to all the academic-related staff, and even occasionally to the chief librarian as well, as at East Anglia and King's College London. Some of these staff also have responsibility for functional tasks in, for example, automation or acquisitions. At Sussex, this subject specialist system is an additional overlay to an essentially functional staff structure without separate subject librarians. A full subject specialization for all members of the academic-related staff is unusual, partly because the number of such staff are often quite low, but also because it is increasingly unrealistic to expect an adequate attention to subject responsibilities from staff whose functional duties are growing in complexity and pressure.

Most libraries, therefore, have a separate group of subject librarians, and where there are other branches their librarians usually act as subject librarians too. In several libraries, this subject organization has been embodied in the design of the main library building; Glasgow is a good example, with a separate subject library on each of its upper floors. At Reading and Southampton, older buildings have been extended and remodeled to allow for subject librarians on each floor. But, since subject librarians are a comparatively recent development in most libraries, quite a few have had to accommodate such staff in areas designed with other aims in mind, or have grouped their subject staff on the entrance floor.

The duties of subject librarians vary as much as their location. They are usually responsible for liaison with specific departments and their library representatives, but the extent of their involvement in collection development varies, even within one library. They may be required to undertake on-line searching, or the library may have one person who specializes in this. They usually give some form of instruction for users, with a wide variation in the amount and level of sophistication. They often classify books and, less usually, catalogue them. They do not usually have other staff under their control, though a clerical assistant sometimes work with them. Above all, they respond to both specialized and routine enquiries from library users within the subject area.

Subject librarians do not usually have well-defined duties or detailed job descriptions, and are often free to develop their own interpretation of their responsibilities. Even within one library, individual subject librarians may work along different lines, within a very loose framework suggested by the chief librarian. In this, they are the library staff most like academics and cannot easily be brought within a strongly hierarchical structure. They can be very valuable in targeting the library's services to different groups of users at a time when the needs of these groups are diverging rapidly, and in developing specialized services to meet particular needs. But there is always the danger that subject coverage will be superficial and spread too thinly, since libraries cannot hope to cover adequately with a few staff all the subjects taught at a university. The idea of subject librarians tends to imply a greater level of subject knowledge (as opposed to knowledge of information sources) than most libraries can provide in all but a few subjects. Newcastle, more realistically, refers to its liaison group, not to its subject librarians. The basic reason for organizing staff by subjects is to maximize the extent to which they can take the library's services and resources into the departments and schools of the university; through them, the library can learn as much as possible about the needs of academics and students in a wide range of subjects, and can promote its own services in response to those needs. It makes sense, then, for libraries to target and promote their services in particular subjects, but not to suggest greater subject knowledge than is actually available.

An argument often advanced against the system of subject librarians is that it offers little basis for promotion, and that the subject librarian is likely to remain in the same post indefinitely. This is proving all too true in the present climate of stagnation among academic-related staff. Some libraries, like Bath and Southampton, are moving instead toward a subject-team approach, by giving the subject librarian a small staff to manage and a greater range of duties to carry out. This means, in effect, creating the equivalent of small branch libraries on the upper floors of the main library. The main difference is that circulation is not usually considered a possible function of the subject team, though it is a major part of the work of branch libraries.

Among the duties devolved, or suggested for devolution, to subject teams is cataloguing. Automated systems have made it possible for cataloging to be carried out anywhere in the library, and the availability of records from external databases has made cataloguing a job for senior library assistants in most libraries. Decentralized cataloguing requires a central team responsible for quality control in libraries like Glasgow and Edinburgh. Inter-library loans have been decentralized in some libraries, as has on-line searching. But only one or two libraries, like Aberdeen, have issue terminals on their upper floors, and none has yet decentralized periodicals check-in in this way, though several libraries are looking at the possibility.

The logical conclusion of this development, given the increasing automation of technical processes in most libraries, is a library where subject teams are responsible for most of these processes, using their own terminals. Technical services departments could then be reduced to small groups coordinating and monitoring the work of the subject teams, and the difficulty of justifying a staff structure with a substantial number of senior staff in technical services could be removed. In many ways, subject teams resemble branch libraries, and both have as their basic purpose an ability to direct specific library services to specific groups of users. Subject teams avoid the major disadvantage of branch libraries, which is their separate location and distance from the main building, and are much less of a hindrance to interdisciplinary studies. If they are organized with enough flexibility and logic, they can respond to changes in the university's subject coverage and emphasis without major reorganization. From the library staff's point of view, subject teams offer more varied work than does a strictly functional organization, and they provide greater scope for academic-related staff to gain management experience without abandoning their subject expertise.

Subject teams are an attractive form of organization in a growing, but still fairly small, number of libraries. But library organizational structures are not just determined by the library's own needs. The demands of the university are also a major influence, especially in a period like the present, when universities are making substantial changes to their own structures and management priorities, chiefly under the guidelines of the Jarratt Report. Universities are demanding from their libraries greater accountability in the use of resources, greater measurable effectiveness and efficiency, more detailed planning, and a more executive management style. The government is demanding these changes from the universities, who are in turn demanding them from what they see as their service organizations, like the library and the computing centre. Subject teams in libraries do not appear to provide a satisfactory means of meeting such demands, which require less emphasis on actual services and more emphasis on the analysis and control of the way in which services are provided. It must be said, however, that the functional and hierarchical type of organization seems equally unsatisfactory as a basis for responding to these demands for accountability.

These demands require a library which is oriented toward management issues and services at the same time. In most libraries, functions such as planning are carried out by the librarian or members of the management team as the need arises. A few libraries have produced staffing plans or financial plans for two or three years ahead, but most have extremely limited planning horizons and plans tend to be produced as a hurried reaction to crises. But an emerging trend assigns specific responsibility for continued planning to a particular person or group, just as universities do. Kent and Newcastle, for example, have a sub-librarian whose duties specifically include planning, while Southampton has a planning and administration division with the librarian as its head. At a time when university funding is becoming linked to the production of detailed strategic plans, it seems advisable for libraries to look carefully at their own ways of planning, and to make better arrangements for coordination and control.

The same advice applies to resource allocation within libraries. As the movement toward one-line, cost-centre budgets grows, decisions on resource allocation in all but the smallest libraries will become too complex for the librarian alone. A senior staff member will be needed to coordinate action and advice in this area, and to be responsible for overall financial control. Almost all libraries currently leave decisions on resource allocation to the librarian, while financial control is usually fragmented among acquisitions librarians, accounts sections, and the librarian or deputy. Newcastle has a sub-librarian for resources and finance, and more libraries are likely to find such a position necessary in the future.

Demands for accountability imply effective managerial control of the library structure and an acceptable system of management information and performance measurement. This system, being mainly derived from automated systems, will increase the pressure to have a senior staff member coordinating automation; some libraries already do this, but others treat automation as a sub-function of technical services or leave it to a junior post with emphasis on the purely technical. Since automated systems are becoming a vital part of most library activities and can influence decision making, specific responsibility for automation must be given to a senior staff member who can make an overview of the needs of the whole library.

Effective managerial control is a much more difficult question. No library has enough senior staff available to coordinate planning, finance, and automation; provide subject-based services of reasonable sophistication; and run a functional hierarchy. These diverse requirements seem to pull in different directions, and it would appear impossible to attain them all without a much larger senior staff. Since at present libraries vary so much in staffing structures, they are likely to respond to demands for effective management by emphasizing the strengths of their current positions. Functional and hierarchical libraries will be able to emphasize the degree of control this gives them, while subject-based libraries with a more fluid structure will stress the effectiveness and quality of their services. Libraries which are a hybrid of these two basic types will probably come under greater pressure to become like one or the other.

The most important requirement, though, is to make adequate provision for proper coordination of planning, resource allocation, and automation, since this is the direction being followed by the universities themselves. Welding this to existing staff structures is made difficult by the inertia of these structures and by the shrinking numbers of senior staff. It looks as though many libraries can only achieve greater coordination of planning and resource allocation at the expense either of less effective control over library processes or of a lower level of services which senior staff can provide. This coordination will have to be achieved by such staff in addition to their previous responsibilities, or by dividing a greater range of duties among a smaller number of staff. These extra demands are inevitable as the universities give their libraries greater freedom to make their own decisions about resource allocation but demand greater accountability in return.

In response to such pressure, libraries are likely to use a team approach to issues and problems which cut across functional and subject-based structures. Permanent or temporary teams of this kind already exist in quite a few libraries. By far the most common are working groups set up to coordinate the implementation of automated systems; Aberdeen, for example, set up eight working groups addressing aspects of its new integrated system. In some cases, as at City, such groups have become permanent, but their existence is usually only temporary. Planning for new accommodation also tends to produce temporary groups. A few libraries have established working groups on other topics which are more likely to be permanent, such as library promotion and income generation, stock management policy, and staff development and training. But hardly any have followed a policy of setting up such groups for a wide range of topics, as Salford and Sheffield have done, and using them as a fundamental part of library organization. None have yet extended group use areas like finance and management, though this is being considered at East Anglia.

There are obvious advantages to establishing groups or teams. Staff are generally pleased to be involved in planning and development of policies, and morale is usually improved. Better use is made of staff knowledge and experience, problems and difficulties can be aired, and there is greater coordination among different sections of the library. But much depends on the role of such working groups in library management. If they are to be more than a temporary exercise intended to boost morale, they ought to be chaired or convened by the librarian, or in larger libraries by a senior staff member with access to the librarian. A suitable balance must be found between staff-elected and librarian-appointed groups, to ensure that the members and their work are acceptable to, and taken seriously by, the library as a whole. A similar balance is needed when assessing the extent to which a group's recommendations and decisions are likely to be followed by the librarian. Despite the Jarratt Report's emphasis on the executive responsibility and power of the librarian as a department head, there is certainly much more scope and need for staff involvement in library-wide issues and planning. This is as much in the librarian's interest as in that of the staff as a whole.

If these teams or working groups also improve morale and produce a greater sense of cohesion and common purpose, they will be of even more value to the library. Many libraries have experienced major problems in morale and communication as a result of recent pressures: continued loss of posts, few new professional staff, lower levels of acquisitions, higher and more varied demands from users, rapid change caused by automation, and uncertainty about the future. These problems are usually recognized and some measures are taken to lessen them, but the efforts are often half-hearted or insufficiently integrated into the daily working lives of the staff. Many libraries hold staff meetings, for example, as a means of improving communication. These meetings are usually infrequent, such as once a term, and are often linked to Library Committee meetings (their main purpose is for the librarian to inform the staff about general developments affecting the library). A common pattern is for there to be one meeting for academic-related staff and another for clerical and other staff. Some libraries include all heads of departments or all professionally qualified staff in their senior staff meetings; a few have elected representatives of the junior staff at senior meetings. In the larger libraries, these meetings are likely to involve as many as 40 staff—too many to be anything more than an audience. The librarian almost always chairs such meetings; it is rare to find a senior staff meeting which elects its own chairman and secretary, as happens at UWIST. Equally rare is a regular meeting of all library staff, even in the smaller libraries, though one is held at Surrey once a year. Large libraries like the Bodleian have separate meetings for different grades of staff. Almost all libraries have many regular meetings of functional divisions and departments, and of subject staff. Also common are meetings for staff at a particular site or group of sites; a multi-site library is another major source of communication problems and is too fragmented for there to be much feeling of unity and common purpose among all its staff.

In addition to meetings, another frequent channel for communication is the staff newsletter, which an increasing number of libraries now produce. Such newsletters have their limitations. They are usually edited by a fairly junior member of staff and appear comparatively infrequently; the Bodleian's weekly newsletter is an exception, made necessary by the size of the library system it serves. Newsletters rarely contain more than factual information about current events in the library and social notes; detailed and authoritative statements about policies and plans by the librarian or a senior member of staff are quite unusual. A more up-to-date and extensive source of information is almost invariably the staff tea-room; in multi-site libraries, for example, it is usually necessary for the site librarian to make a regular appearance in the tea-room of the main library, to be sure of keeping up with library developments. For in spite of meetings and newsletters, most libraries—whatever their size—have major problems with communication, and informal channels are usually much more effective than formal ones. There are many reasons for this; among the most important are too little time for senior staff to give their attention to communication, an unwillingness or lack of awareness on their part, and organizational structures which make communication more difficult. The team approach can improve this, but effective communication is above all a question of sufficient time, priority, and willingness among senior staff. At a time when staff morale is generally fairly low and rapid change is taking place in libraries, communication has a vital role in the successful development and adaptation of university libraries.

Equally vital is staff training and development. Most libraries have a staff member specifically responsible for this area, though usually in addition to other major responsibilities. But because of lack of time and funds, training is often limited mainly to teaching new junior staff the details of their job and perhaps giving new staff an introduction to the library as a whole. Trainee library assistants undertaking their year's work experience before studying librarianship are usually given a training programme which involves rotating through various library departments; this is a requirement for trainees under SCONUL's scheme. But other new staff are unlikely to receive such a broadly based training. Indeed, several libraries object to this need for trainee rotation, and quite a few abolished such trainee posts in the aftermath of the 1981 cuts.

Training for professionally qualified staff is mainly a matter of continuing professional development. This is usually left to the initiative of the individual. Fewer funds than ever are available for staff to attend conferences or courses, but several libraries have managed to arrange exchanges for one or two of their academic-related staff. These exchanges are usually with the United States or Canada, though France is now a possibility. Study leave is occasionally granted to senior staff. There is a major problem with professionally qualified staff on senior clerical grades who have much less opportunity and comparatively little incentive for professional development, despite their qualifications and their potential to benefit from continuing education. Even among the most senior academic-related staff, there is no formal training in library management, though a step in the right direction was made with a seminar in 1986 for new chief librarians to exchange experiences and learn from each other.

In general, few libraries have a systematic programme of training and continuing education for their staff. Even for those who do, like Surrey, the low turnover of permanent staff soon makes it difficult to keep people interested and to find new topics to cover. Formal staff assessment and appraisal will make a difference, however, since staff development and career paths are an essential aspect of a good appraisal system. Those libraries which now undertake informal appraisal sometimes include continuing education already. Whether attention to the development of individual staff members will do much to improve morale will depend on a library's ability to offer its staff rewarding and satisfying careers.

At present, libraries have major problems with morale because of professional stagnation, continuing staffing reductions, and uncertainty about the future. Current arrangements for communication and training offer little scope for improvement. At the same time, libraries are in the midst of substantial organizational restructuring, partly because of losses of senior posts, partly as a reaction to changing management requirements in the universities, and partly because of automation. All this is a management challenge of major proportions, and the future effectiveness of university libraries depends to a large extent on their response to it.

REFERENCES

1. *University statistics, vol. 3, Finance*, 1980/81-1984/85; *Statistics of education, vol. 6, Universities*, 1979/80.
2. SCONUL. *University library expenditure statistics* 1984/85, p. 4-5.
3. *University statistics, vol. 3, Finance*, 1980/81-1984/85.
4. *University statistics, vol. 3, Finance* gives male and female numbers of academic-related staff.
5. *University statistics, vol. 3, Finance*, 1980/81-1984/85.

Chapter 4

Collections

The rate of growth of university library collections was reduced sharply in the 1980s. Three-quarters of the libraries surveyed by SCONUL bought fewer monographs and subscribed to fewer periodicals in 1984/85 than they had in 1979/80. The cuts fell harder on monographs; the most common reduction was between 19% and 27%, though several libraries reported a cut of over 40%. Periodical subscriptions were predominantly reduced by up to 13%, but quite a few libraries cut their number of subscriptions by more than this. Further reductions were made in 1985/86, with 32% of libraries cutting periodical subscriptions and 38% cutting monograph purchases.[1] Within this general picture, there were considerable individual variations and fluctuations from year to year, but the overall trend is very clear. University libraries, on the whole, have a substantially smaller number of periodical subscriptions than they used to, and buy markedly fewer monographs.

A glance at almost any series of annual reports illustrates this decline. The number of volumes added to the library at Brunel averaged 9,500 a year between 1981 and 1986, compared with 12,250 between 1977 and 1980 and 14,000 between 1973 and 1976. At Dundee, the number of new accessions in 1984/85 was less than half what it had been in 1982/83. St Andrews bought 40% fewer monographs in 1985/86 than in 1982/83. Swansea added 27% fewer books in 1985/86 than in 1980/81, and reduced periodical subscriptions by 11% between 1982/83 and 1985/86. At Reading, the number of monographs bought fell by 39% from 1978/79 to 1982/83, and has fallen further since then; the decline from nearly 14,000 monographs to less than 6,000 was a major factor in the combination of book orders and cataloguing into a jointly staffed department. A similar decline at Kent contributed to the merging of previously separate monographs and serials departments.

Recurrent expenditure on books and periodicals rose 40% between 1980/81 and 1984/85, in cash terms.[2] But this conceals a shift from expenditure on staff to expenditure on materials, as the share of total recurrent expenditure which went on books and periodicals rose from 29% to 39%. The figures also conceal a much greater increase in expenditure on periodicals, which grew by 59% compared with 27% for books. And within this overall increase, most libraries suffered actual cash decreases in expenditures on materials, in some year. In 1981/82, at least 17 libraries (excluding those in London) spent less in cash terms on books and periodicals than they had in the previous year. Virtually all these cash cuts were in book expenditures; 14 libraries (again excluding those in London) actually spent less on books in 1984/85 than they had five years earlier, in 1980/81. All libraries were spending more by then on periodicals; even in the worse year for cuts, 1981/82, only eight libraries spent less in cash on periodicals than they had in 1980/81.

Cash expenditure on books fluctuated greatly in individual libraries during this five-year period. Only four (Leeds, Newcastle, Oxford, and Cambridge) managed to maintain a continuous rise. Excluding the London libraries, a total of 17 libraries averaged less cash expenditure a year over the five years than they had spent in 1980/81. In some cases, like City and Stirling, the average book expenditure during this period was 25% lower than in 1980/81. The list was dominated by new and technological universities and the Welsh colleges, but it did include larger and older libraries like Hull, Liverpool, Nottingham, and Reading. Falls in cash expenditure on books were most common in 1981/82, when almost 70% of libraries were affected. Only 15% spent less in 1982/83 than they had the year before, but most of these had already been cut in 1981/82. The proportion of libraries cutting expenditure then grew again, with 37% in 1983/84 and 48% in 1984/85.

The full seriousness of these figures becomes apparent when rates of inflation are taken into account. There are methodological problems here, though, since none of the national indices of prices for books and periodicals is entirely satisfactory. The Index of University Costs, produced for the CVCP, contains a section for books, periodicals, and binding, but SCONUL has argued that it consistently understates price rises by concentrating on books actually bought by libraries, at a time when they are less likely to buy more expensive research titles or hardback copies. SCONUL is also concerned that proper weight should be given to variations in costs across different subject fields and to purchases from foreign countries. It has also suggested that the size of the sample used to measure periodical price rises be increased considerably. Another index produced for prices of academic books by the Centre for Library and Information Management (CLAIM) also understated the level of inflation in 1983 and 1984, by omitting books which were unpriced in BNB. Since 1985, CLAIM (now the Library and Information Statistics Unit) has begun a new series of indices for average prices of British and American academic books, based on data from Blackwell. A periodicals price index is also published by Blackwell alone; again, there is uncertainty about the size of the sample, which is likely to be greatly expanded in the future.[3] There are other more general indices which do not relate specifically to academic publications; among these is the government's retail price index for books, newspapers, and periodicals.

These measurements of average price rises should therefore be used with caution, since they almost certainly understate the extent of such rises. Nevertheless, even with these reservations, it is clear that library expenditure on materials has fallen considerably in real terms. The comparison in Figure 4.1 is based on the UGC's statistics of library expenditure and the Index of University Costs.

The increasing gap between the two indices illustrates the decline in the purchasing power of library materials budgets, which fell by 21% in this period (see Table 2.2, p. 42). It is also interesting to compare the index of costs with expenditure in particular libraries, as in Figure 4.2, which uses three libraries of different types.

There is a clear gap between costs and expenditure, even in the index for Newcastle, which was one of the few libraries to record a continuous rise in cash expenditure during this period. Salford was one of the worst-affected libraries; its expenditure was only 3% higher at the end of the period, though prices had risen by almost 70%. Most other libraries lay somewhere between these two and suffered one or more falls in expenditure, as in the index for Read-

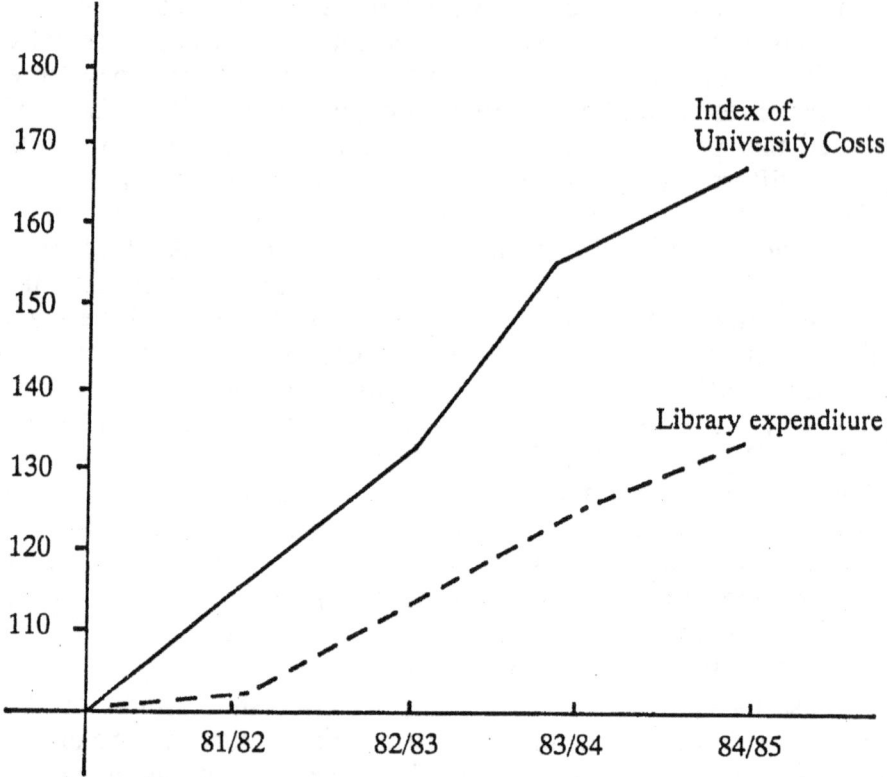

FIGURE 4.1. Index of University costs compared with library recurrent expenditure on books, periodicals and binding (1980/81 = 100).

ing. When these trends in expenditure are shown in real terms, the decline in the value of library budgets is dramatic (Figure 4.3).

The fall in real terms in 1981/82 was sharp and severe, especially in those libraries which suffered a decrease in cash expenditure. Salford had the real value of its materials budget cut by 40%, and many libraries lost more than the average 13%. Since then, the decline has continued for most libraries; only a few have managed to record an increase in real terms, usually only for one year at a time. It must be emphasized again that the basis for this calculation is the Index of University Costs, which almost certainly understates the rate of price rises. The true decline in real terms is likely to have been even worse.

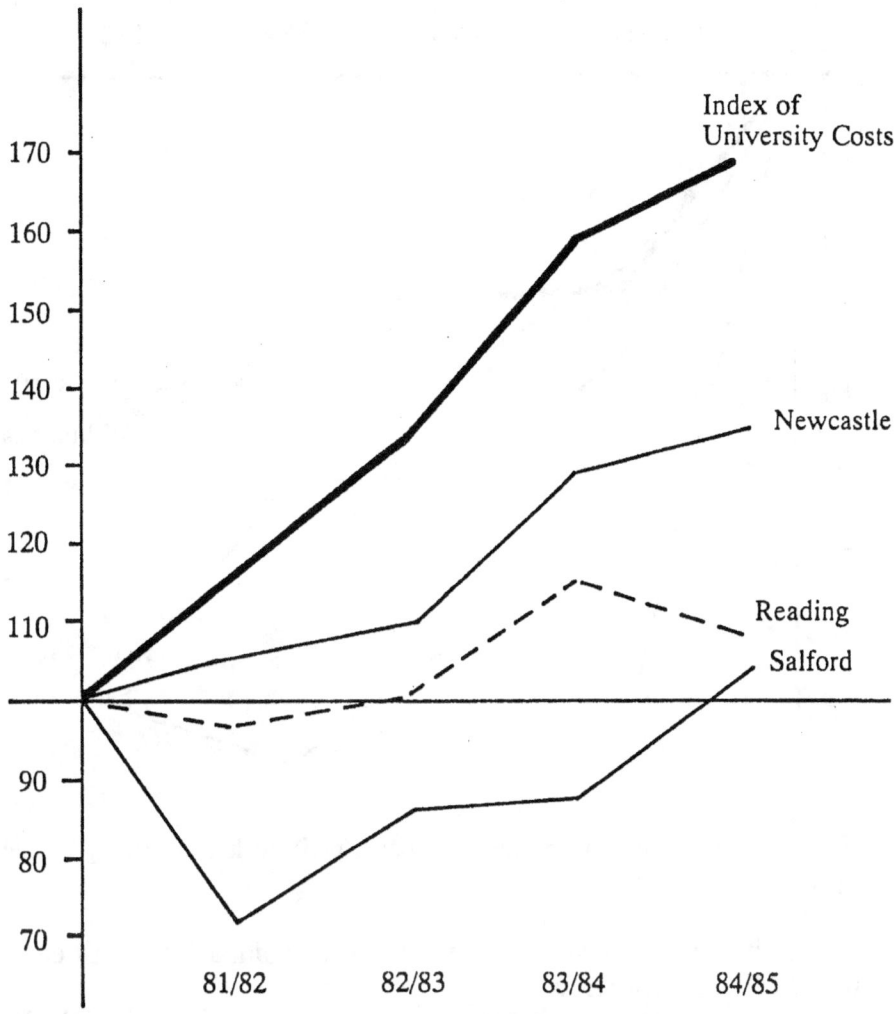

FIGURE 4.2. Indices of recurrent expenditure on books, periodicals and binding (1980/81 = 100).

Periodicals expenditure can be measured against the Blackwell index, which is generally considered to be reasonably accurate, though fairly narrowly based. Periodical prices rose 92% between 1980/81 and 1984/85, according to this index, while library expenditure on periodicals rose only 59%. Individual libraries varied

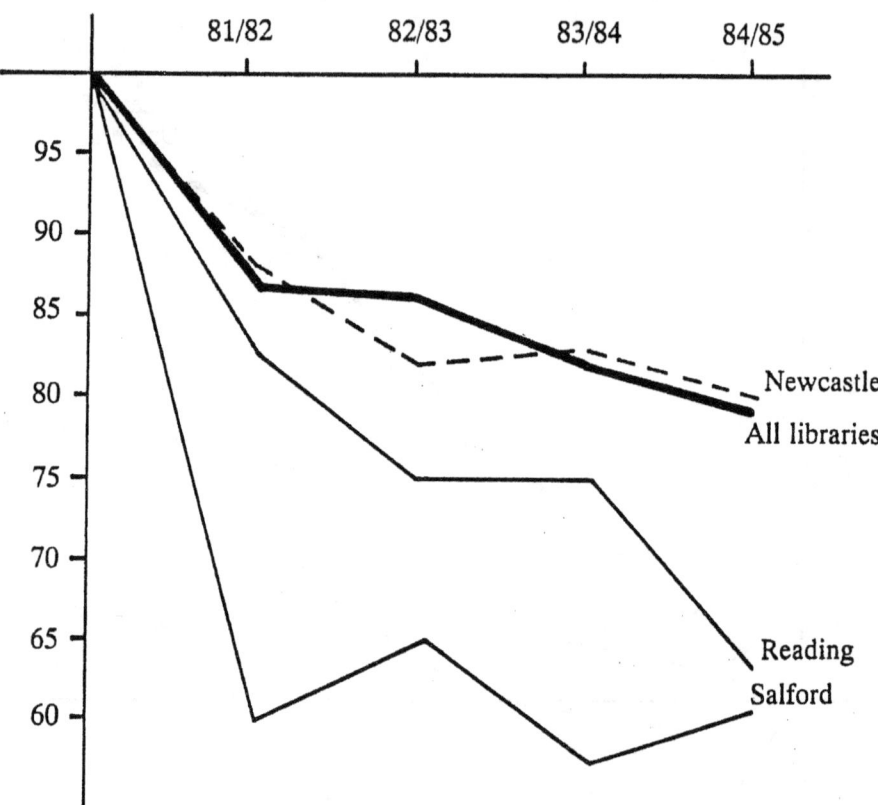

FIGURE 4.3. Recurrent expenditure on books, periodicals and binding in real terms (1980/81 = 100).

considerably, both from year to year and in comparison with each other, as Figure 4.4 shows.

These figures can also be shown in real terms, using the Blackwell index. The individual variations reflect the timing of cancellation exercises and libraries' efforts to protect periodicals subscriptions. But the overall trend is a clear and continuing decline in expenditure on periodicals in real terms (Figure 4.5).

Trends in book expenditure are harder to measure, partly because of the lack of satisfactory indices, and partly because of considerable variations from year to year in particular libraries. Figure 4.6 shows cash expenditure on books between 1980/81 and 1984/85, for all British university libraries and for the three sample libraries. Also

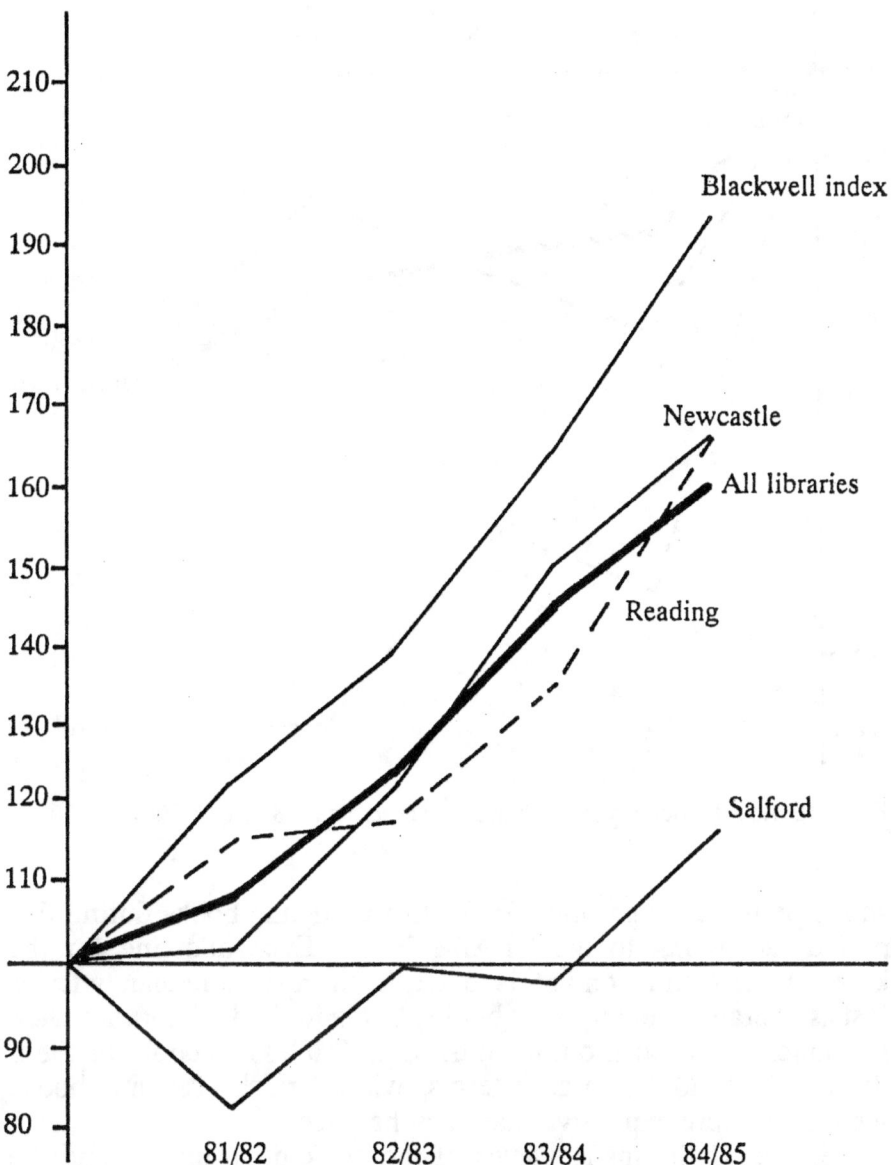

FIGURE 4.4. Indices of expenditures on periodicals (1980/81 = 100).

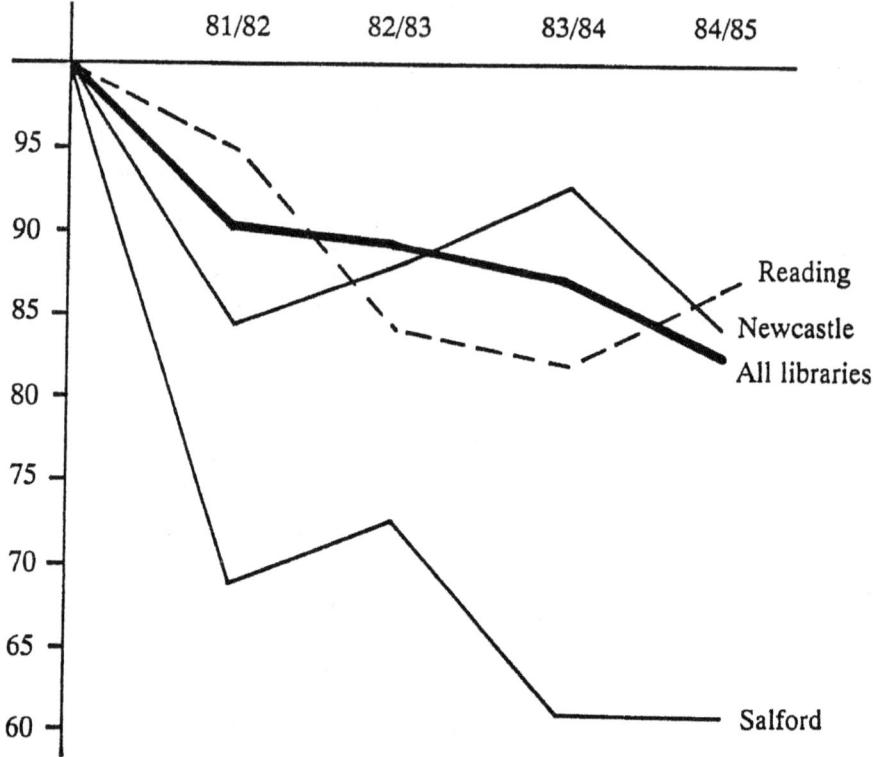

FIGURE 4.5. Periodicals expenditure in real terms (1980/81 = 100).

shown is the average price for British academic books during this period, according to the CLAIM index. Even allowing for the known underestimation in this index, it still rose more than twice as fast as overall expenditure on books. Some individual libraries were in a much worse position; Reading spent 8% less on books in 1984/85 than in 1980/81, in cash terms, while British academic books were 57% more expensive than they had been.

Because of the inadequacies of the book price indices and the impossibility of calculating a meaningful weighting to allow for the different countries of origin of academic books, book expenditure in real terms cannot be measured with any accuracy. But, given that many libraries were forced to cut expenditure in cash terms during this period, there was undoubtedly an even greater fall in real terms.

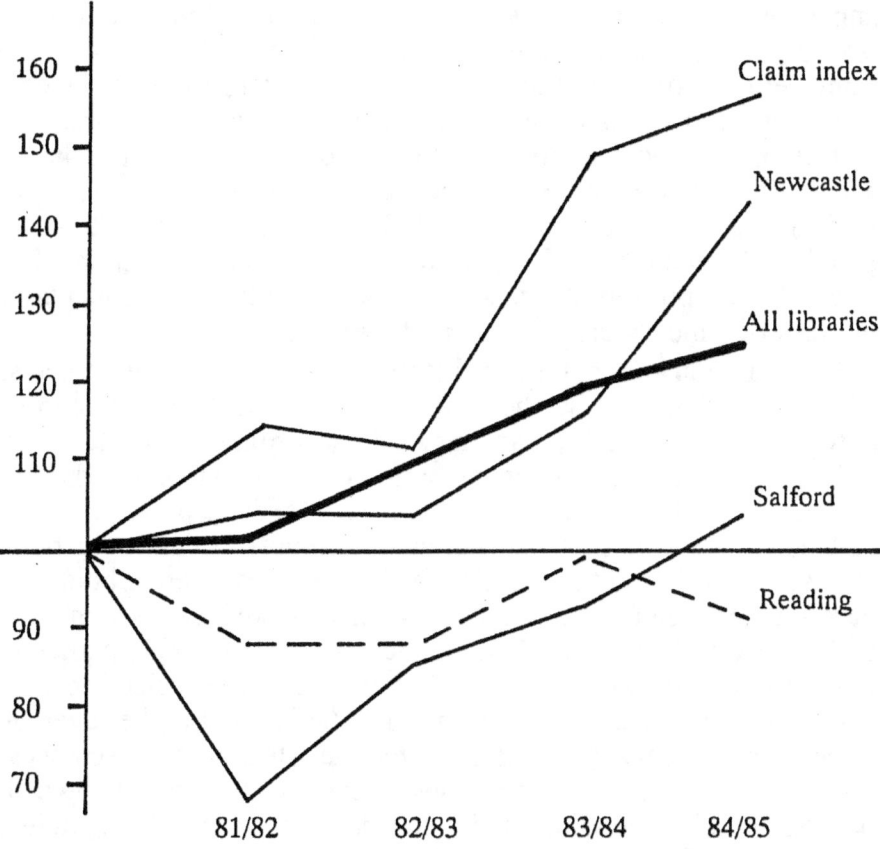

FIGURE 4.6. Indices of expenditure on books (1980/81 = 100).

It is reasonable to conclude that this decline in real expenditure was sharper and more severe than the decline for periodicals purchase. One estimate of this decline puts it at over 34% between 1981 and 1987, and 12.6% between 1985 and 1987.[4]

The decline in the value of library budgets must be seen in terms of the effect of overseas purchases and subject variations. A substantial proportion of the books and periodicals bought by most university libraries comes from overseas and depends directly or indirectly on the value of the pound for its cost. The cuts from 1981 coincided with a sharp fall in the pound; between 1981 and 1985, its annual average value against the American dollar fell by a total of over 35%. Against the German mark, the pound fell by 17% in the same period. For many libraries this added considerably to the cost of perhaps 20 to 50% of their books and periodicals, or in the case of Cambridge and the Bodleian to the cost of all their purchased acquisitions. The Blackwell index showed that North American periodicals rose in price by about 150% between 1981 and 1985, compared with about 50% for periodicals published in Britain. The higher the proportion of overseas material in a library's collection, the faster its individual rate of inflation rose.

Price rises also occurred at different rates in different subjects. The average cost of periodicals in science and technology doubled between 1981 and 1985, reaching £160, according to the Blackwell index. Arts and social sciences periodicals rose more slowly and averaged less than a quarter of this price. Medical periodicals fell between these two groups. Similar differences occurred in book prices. According to the CLAIM index, British academic books on pure science rose 63% in price between 1981 and 1985, compared with an overall average of 56%; they were about 60% higher in price than the overall average. A library which emphasized science and technology faced a steeper rate of inflation and higher average prices than a library which emphasized the arts and social sciences. Libraries which collected in all these areas found an increasing proportion of their expenditure going to science and technology, unless specially weighted cuts were made to reverse this trend.

A similar shift took place with periodicals. Some libraries, like Southampton, followed a policy of protecting periodicals and allowing the proportion of expenditure on books to fall. This policy was often determined by the academic staff; at Surrey, the Library Committee decided to let the proportion spent on periodicals to rise from 50% to 67% during this period. At Reading in 1986/87, the Committee of Deans decided that a proposed cut of 11% in the materials budget should fall on books. Even without such academic policies, the periodicals share of library expenditure grew inexorably, unless cancellation exercises were undertaken to reduce it. Over Britain as a whole, the ratio of periodicals to books rose from 48.8:51.2 to 54.4:45.6, according to the UGC statistics. This conceals considerable variations between libraries. In SCONUL's figures, the median value in 1984/85 for periodicals as a proportion of the acquisitions budget was 58.1% in the United Kingdom, compared with 55.2% in 1981/82.[5] Several libraries were spending over 70% of their acquisitions budget on periodicals, including Keele with 79.7%, and many were spending between 60 and 70%. This was despite, in most cases, one or more cancellation exercises since 1981/82. There was little difference between types of library, though the median value in the old Scottish universities and the Welsh colleges was over 60%.

These, then, are the trends evident in published statistics for the earlier 1980s. In subsequent years, the general picture has not changed greatly. Almost all libraries are still suffering considerable reductions in real terms, and some, like Hull and Sussex, are being cut in cash terms as well. The inflation rate for periodicals seems to have slowed a little, with the Blackwell index rising 9.3% in 1986, 12.3% in 1987, and 6.2% in 1988. The pound has risen in value against the American dollar, to the extent that North American periodicals rose an average of only 1.4% in 1987, and not at all in 1988. But against other currencies, especially in Europe, the pound has continued to be weak; the Blackwell index for 1987 put the rise in periodicals from outside Britain and North America at 34.3%. The drift towards periodicals continues, with more libraries (such as Reading and King's College London) spending nearly 80% of their budget on them.

The differences between libraries are becoming more marked, as the effects of the UGC's new selective funding filter through to acquisitions budgets. Libraries whose universities are benefiting most from the UGC's formula are generally much better placed than those whose parent institution has been in the "safety net." Only a handful of libraries can feel reasonably optimistic that their current budget contains an adequate increase when inflation rates are considered. For most, the immediate prospect is a greater or smaller decline in real terms, in continuation of the trend begun in 1980/81.

One new factor has been the UGC's special allocation of £3 million to university libraries in each of the years 1987/88 to 1989/90. This money was distributed in proportion to the student numbers of each institution, rather than in accordance with the new formula for allocating university block grants. For most libraries, this special grant was about 10% of their 1986/87 budget for books and periodicals, and was therefore a substantial addition. It is likely that some universities will reduce their libraries' recurrent grants on the grounds that some or all of the special allocation will make up the difference. At Hull and Sussex, the extra funds were used to lessen the size of a cut in library funding during the period 1987/88-1989/90. But most libraries will receive the special allocation on top of their recurrent budget, as the UGC intended. There is a strong temptation to use the additional funds to maintain existing periodical subscriptions or start new ones, in view of the continuing pressure on periodicals budgets. But the special allocation is for three years only, and its intended use is to fill gaps in monograph collections and periodical back runs, rather than to boost the level of recurrent expenditure on new materials.

This special allocation from the UGC is an admission that considerable harm has been done to collections in British university libraries since the cuts of 1981/82. But for all the statistics on expenditure and accessions, it is very difficult to assess the extent and nature of this damage. Undoubtedly libraries have had to be much more selective about what they buy, and their collections have a much more narrow coverage of 1980s material than they had for the 1970s. Only about a half dozen libraries have been able to claim the status of a continuing research collection, in the sense of acquiring materials in such depth and breadth as to support research in almost any academic subject. A few of the smaller, technological university libraries have never aspired to more than provision for a fairly narrow range of current needs. The other libraries, the majority, have fallen somewhere between these two extremes. It is they who have been most affected by the decline in the value of acquisitions budgets, and it is their ability to support potential research needs in a fairly broad range of subjects which has been all but destroyed. This shrinking horizon will continue for most of these libraries in the immediate future, reducing their collections of current material to the level of undergraduate study with only a thin overlay for specific current research needs.

This contraction and mandatory selectivity in collection-building has occurred in a period when the so-called "information explosion" has continued unabated. The number of periodicals being published in still rising dramatically, with new titles being continually announced. Between 1976 and 1985, according to one survey of eight major publishers, there was an increase of over 120% in the number of scholarly journals they published. One major American periodicals supplier handled 99,000 active titles in 1987, a rise of about 160% since 1974.[6] Yet most university libraries are faced with a continually shrinking periodicals collection, and can only add new titles to it at the expense of one or more existing subscriptions. The fall in numbers of periodicals taken is estimated at more than 14% between 1981 and 1987. Nor is there any sign of reduction in the number of new academic books being published, though university libraries bought 35% fewer books in 1987 than in 1981.[7]

British university libraries acquired an ever smaller proportion of the scholarly books and periodicals being published. In general terms, their collections are therefore of increasingly less value for meeting current research needs, let alone possible future needs, given that research is a cumulative process which builds on existing documented research, and that most universities have done little to reduce the range and scope of the research they carry out. A more specific assessment of the value of library collections for research is a qualitative question, which must rely mainly on the opinions of academic researchers. Steps have been taken to find out these opinions in a formal and systematic way. The British Library commissioned a survey of university academic staff, to see whether they felt that the value of research collections in the university libraries and the British Library had declined.[8] Many academic felt that their research had suffered because of the growing difficulty in obtaining up-to-date material. There was considerable evidence that more academic staff were bypassing their university libraries and relying more heavily on personal contacts and less formal means of sharing the results of research.

SCONUL has approached learned societies, such as the Royal Society and the British Academy, to find out their members' views. It has also asked university libraries to consult research committees and faculty deans in their universities. Informal assessment by academics of the research value of library collections abounds in all universities, but almost all of this appears as a reaction to cuts of particular journals or sharp reductions in book allocations. Academic opinion rarely takes a broader perspective on the adequacy of library collections.

Libraries have only recently begun to make their own formal assessments of their collections. The method known as Conspectus, developed by the Research Libraries Group in the United States, has been used by the British library and the eight Scottish university libraries. Conspectus enables the recording of existing collections levels in specific subjects as well as the current level of acquisition, but its main weakness is the strong element of subjective assessment involved. The subject arrangement imposed by the Library of Congress classification is sometimes inconsistent and overlapping. Several of the Scottish libraries have found it difficult to apply in practice. Nevertheless, Conspectus is the only realistic choice for formal assessment of collections and provides a good basis for revealing a library's strengths and weaknesses, especially in comparison with other libraries.

British university libraries do not have detailed written guidelines for collecting in particular subject areas, so Conspectus is also likely to be valuable for prompting a reappraisal and formalizing of collection development policies. At a time when funds for books and periodicals are under such pressure, more formal and detailed policies will help to direct more selective acquisition to areas of highest priority. The absence of these formal guidelines until now can be traced, in large part, to the dominance of academic staff in the selection of library materials. Indeed, at present such formal policies would have to be written by academic staff rather than librarians, in most libraries. At Southampton this is already taking place, and departments are in the process of producing policy statements using forms similar to those of Conspectus.

Book selection in many libraries is basically the responsibility of the academic staff, often coordinated by a system of departmental library liaison officers. At Oxford, an even more formal approach is used for the Bodleian and the faculty libraries, with faculty library committees making decisions on book selection. The involvement of library staff varies from library to library, and from subject to subject, though they are always able to select reference tools. In some libraries, subject specialists have little or no say in book selection for their subjects, but in most libraries at least some of the subject specialists are actively involved in selecting material. Only in a few libraries (including such diverse types as Cambridge, City, and Sussex) is most of the book selection undertaken by library staff.

Librarians are much more likely to be responsible for ensuring that sufficient quantities of student textbooks and books on reading lists are available. There is often a separate fund for such purchases, distinct from funds assigned to departmental recommendations. Reading lists are used as the basis for buying this kind of material, supplemented by some monitoring of book use in the Short Loan or Reserve Collections. Some libraries are using their automated circulation systems to pinpoint books in high demand for the possible purchase of extra copies. Sussex has probably gone furthest in this direction by setting up a Course Provision Section. Its duties include gathering and processing reading lists, acquiring multiple copies, and managing the Short Loan and Reserve Collections. It makes use of the ability of an adapted Geac circulation system to show the total uses of a book since it was catalogued and its uses over the previous six terms. Up to 25% of the book budget can be spent on multiple copies. At a time when academics are increasing their control over library book funds, it is very important for libraries to protect and make provision for the majority of their users, the undergraduates, who have also been hit by sharply rising book prices and a fall in the real value of student grants. Special arrangements to meet their needs for textbooks and multiple copies are increasingly necessary.

Sussex has also used its circulation system to guide its general collecting policies.[9] In each of 35 subject groups, the extent to which new books are borrowed within their first year in the library has been calculated, and the results used to direct acquisitions to the more heavily used areas. A check is made by analysing loans to academic staff and research students according to subject. Even in libraries where academics rather than librarians do most of the book selection (unlike Sussex), this kind of information is valuable as a pointer to the immediate usefulness of new books. It is necessary, of course, to use such figures with caution, since they do not take into account factors like use in the library and fluctuations in research activity. But a much closer link between acquisitions and immediate use is now inevitable for most libraries, given that book funds are now too low to be spent on material which may only be used at some time in the future. Only the largest research libraries now have sufficient funds for this wider goal. However unpalatable this is to smaller libraries which had as their ideal the building of collections of value to posterity as well as the present, the decline in funds is forcing them to set strict priorities in their acquisitions, and has made it difficult even to meet current needs. In such a situation, libraries have to rely increasingly on measurements of use, as well as narrowly defined collecting policies, to ensure that their limited funds are distributed in the best way.

A similar process is occurring with periodicals collections. The decline in funding in the 1980s fell heavily on collections which were mostly built up in an unplanned, haphazard way. Among the obvious immediate reactions were to cancel duplicate subscriptions and to place a moratorium on new subscriptions, unless existing ones of the same value could be cancelled. In some universities, departments were allowed to pay for new periodicals out of their share of monograph funds. These measures went hand-in-hand with cancellation exercises, as it became necessary to reduce the basic number of subscriptions if there was to be any money for books. Given that periodicals were the first call on the acquisitions budget, they would soon consume the whole amount available if no corrective action was taken. Consequently, cancellations on a considerable scale were undertaken in almost all libraries, often over several years.

These cancellations were often decided by sending lists of relevant titles to particular departments or schools, and asking them to suggest those which could be cancelled. The target was given either as a percentage of the total value of the list or as a sum in pounds; the most recent price was included for each title on the list. Academics might be asked to meet several different targets, such as 10%, 20%, or 30% reductions, if the final savings required were not known for certain. A common alternative was to ask departments to rank titles on their list and then to cancel the lowest ranked. Both ranking titles and setting targets presented considerable methodological problems, one of the most important being the handling of general and interdisciplinary titles. A substantial amount of record-keeping by the library was also necessary; recently many libraries have taken to building up a database of titles, prices, and departmental interest. But the major problem was usually the bad feeling which cancellation exercises created among the academic staff. Reaching agreement on a final list of cancellations acceptable to the university as a whole was usually a slow and difficult business, tied up with academic decision making and politics. Some librarians had to resort to giving academics an ultimatum and threatening to go ahead with cancellations decided by the library if no agreement could be reached. Even when libraries paid considerable attention to public relations, cancellation exercises were often a traumatic process, though their repetition tended to diminish the trauma.

For all this effort, not to mention the substantial extra work for library staff, the result was only a cheaper periodicals collection, not a better one. Cancellations carried out in this way are not selective, and perpetuate the haphazard nature of a collection built up in times of greater funds. No provision is made for relevant new titles to be added to the collection. Libraries are finding it necessary to review their whole list of subscriptions from this wider perspective, and to make collection assessment and improvement the goal within a much reduced financial framework. Two predominant methods are being used for this: a full-scale rebuilding of the collection, and greater attention to the use made of the existing collection.

Use in the library must be measured in a rough and sketchy way at best, given the constraints on time, staffing, and funding which all libraries face. Two methods commonly used in university libraries at present are to measure the frequency of re-shelving or to ask users to sign a form or label on the volume. Deliberate bias is a possibility in both cases, and can probably be best avoided by giving the survey as little publicity as possible. The results of such surveys can be used not to suggest individual titles for cancellation, but to distinguish core titles from marginal ones. The latter category can then be reviewed as a whole, by comparison with potential additions to the collection. Use studies of these types have been directed to specific subject areas, rather than the whole range of periodicals, and the results are passed to relevant departments for their consideration.

The other method of assessing a periodicals collection involves reviewing it in its entirety. In its simplest form, this can be achieved by assigning each faculty or department an amount of money and asking it to select titles up to that value. This has occasionally been done instead of the more standard cancellation exercise. It is also implicit in the method used by some libraries for dividing acquisitions budgets, when faculties are given a single sum for all purchases, to be used as they think fit. But the best-known example of the wholesale review is the "election" method developed at Sussex; it has since been used at East Anglia and Aston. This has as its basis the idea that each member of the academic staff is given 100 votes, which can be assigned to any title or broken down between several titles, depending on the academic's perception of the value of specific periodicals to his or her work. The library deliberately gives little advice or assistance to academics, though Sussex did provide general and specific subject lists of titles. The analysis of thousands of votes really requires a computer software package capable of manipulating the data according to the number of votes for each title, the number of persons voting for it, and its cost. Current titles with no votes become the basis for a list of proposed cancellations, though this must still be checked with departments. In the place of these cancelled titles, the library can subscribe to new or previously cancelled periodicals with the highest number of votes, depending on the amount of money available. This method depends entirely on subjective assessment by individual academics, with no uniform criteria for assigning votes. The response rate at Sussex and Aston was about 65%, and 71% at East Anglia. Cross-checking against inter-library loan requests for new titles and measurements of use for current titles is essential to reduce this dependence on subjective assessment.

The result is a considerably altered periodicals collection. At Aston, over 200 titles were cancelled, 83 new titles were added, and 32 previously cancelled titles were reinstated, in a collection of less than 1,600 titles. East Anglia cancelled 250 titles and added 70 new ones. The changes at Sussex were less dramatic, but still substantial. The restructured collection then reflects more closely the current research needs of academics, and the library abandons by implication any attempt to preserve long, unbroken runs of periodicals to meet potential future needs. This is parallel to basing book purchases on recent measurements of use. Both approaches are aimed at building a collection which is tailored to current needs, rather than fulfilling any long-term goal of preserving an intellectual heritage for the benefit of future researchers. As the value of library budgets continues to decrease, this kind of approach is likely to spread to all but the largest libraries.

To be effective tailoring the collection to current needs must be continuous, enabling the library to respond to changes of emphasis in a university's teaching and research. A full-scale periodicals review is too cumbersome and time-consuming to be carried out frequently, even in the smallest university libraries. Other ways must then be found to continually monitor the relevance of the periodicals collection, though libraries have not yet gone very far in this direction. One example is Loughborough's Serials Review Group, with academics and librarians as members, which carries out an annual review of the overall health of the collection, at least in a financial sense. Without some form of regular review, it is almost impossible for librarians to respond to demands for different periodicals that reflect changes in courses and research.

These changes in university subject coverage are becoming more frequent and more drastic, and greater selectivity and rationalization are likely in the immediate future. With limited collection development, university libraries are facing a growing challenge to adapt their acquisitions to meet this change. Many libraries have access to some form of funding to assist in the initial buildup of material to support new courses. At Liverpool, for example, new academic developments are provided for on the basis of an initial booklist, supplemented by an extra recurrent amount of 20-30% of the value of the list. But most grants are intended to meet only the initial expenses, leaving the library to find recurrent funds by adjusting priorities within its book fund.

The converse of this lies in making provision for subjects and courses which are no longer taught or researched, an increasingly frequent occurrence in recent years. In several cases, libraries have transferred whole subject areas to another university, following the transfer of a department under a scheme for rationalization. Lancaster, for example, transferred its collection of Central European material to Glasgow and Aberdeen transferred its Scandinavian collection to Edinburgh. Russian collections were transferred from several libraries. More libraries are beginning to weed their older stock, though this is usually confined to removing superseded editions and duplicate copies. Some libraries have assigned staff to stock management sections responsible for weeding, amongst other things. But in general, libraries have yet to tackle on a large scale the adaptation of their existing collections to current needs. Until now, only new acquisitions have been affected by the narrowing scope of collecting policies.

Underlying these changes in the development and assessment of collections in university libraries is a shift in the way funds are allocated to different subjects. This allocation falls into two broad types. The first, and older, type is still used by a majority of libraries. The initial division is into funds for books and funds for periodicals, and is either built into the budget or made by the librarian, usually with the agreement of the Library Committee. Periodicals funds are determined incrementally as the amount needed to meet estimated current commitments, and are not divided among faculties or departments. Funds for monographs are then usually divided between departments according to existing, historical proportions. Some allowance is made for new developments and changing priorities. A few libraries use formulae to divide up some or most of their monograph funds. Others make only notional divisions of monograph funds, which are not revealed to departments. The usual practice, though, is for fixed, public allocations on a largely historical basis.

The other allocation pattern casts the initial division among faculties. A subsequent division is made among departments, giving each a lump sum for books and periodicals. It is the responsibility of the departments, or occasionally the faculties, to decide the relative proportions for books and periodicals. Some libraries, like Bath, UWIST, and Edinburgh, take this a step further by including provision for on-line searching and/or inter-library loans in the sum allocated to faculties. Academic staff can then set priorities for all four categories of expenditure from a single initial allocation. The usual practice is for the library to retain a central fund to meet needs in reference and bibliography, librarianship, and student textbooks.

The initial division among faculties is often made by a committee: the Library Committee at Bath, the Management Sub-Committee of the Library Committee at Edinburgh, and the Academic Services Committee (which absorbed the Library Committee) at Liverpool. The faculties are often responsible for further division among departments; their own library committees develop a variety of ways for doing this. But sometimes this division among departments is also determined by the librarian and a central committee.

Formulae are almost always used when the whole acquisitions budget is divided among departments, but these formulae differ in the variables they contain. Student and staff numbers, and the average cost of books and periodicals are commonly used. Some libraries set a "floor" or minimum amount for each department's share, and several include some allowance for historical factors. The greatest variation is in the provision made for the differing degrees to which subjects depend on the library in their teaching and research, the "coefficient of library dependence" as St Andrews calls it. This can appear as a subject weighting assigned by the library's subject specialists, as at Bradford, or as a factor for books per student, as at Buckingham. Cardiff uses a loans factor calculated from circulation statistics. A related, but rarely used, weighting is for the extent to which studying or researching different subjects requires more books or periodicals in the library. But the most important factor is probably the political balance of subjects within the university, and many libraries have had to tinker with the allocations resulting from their formulae, in order to make them politically acceptable.

Distributing an amount among departments according to a formula is being increasingly used in university libraries. Its introduction is often at the request of academic staff, as happened recently at Southampton. At Hull, the university is hoping that the introduction of this type of formula distribution will provide a model for distributing university funds among departments. Historically based allocations, in contrast, are seen as not reflecting changes in university priorities and as not giving "fair" shares to certain departments. Nevertheless, formulae also cause major disagreements within the university and revisions are constantly being sought. Allocation of funds to subjects is bound up with university politics, especially at a time when the total to be shared is continually decreasing. The advantage of the formula distribution is that it deflects the pressure to justify allocations away from the librarian personally, and toward a series of committees.

The pressure to justify periodicals cancellations is also lessened. Under the formula distribution, it is the departments' responsibility to keep their periodicals list within the scope of the budget; at UWIST, for example, any overspending is automatically taken from a department's own funds. The library usually provides an annual estimate of next year's commitments for periodicals to each department, in time for cancellations to be made if necessary. Some libraries insist on a maximum level for periodicals expenditure within each department's allocation, such as 80% or 85%, to give protection against underestimating the rise in prices. Cancellations become the annual responsibility of the departments, rather than a major exercise for the whole library.

The growing trend toward giving departments greater control of their share of the library's budget is closely linked to collecting policies' being directed at current and immediate needs. They are part of a reaction—perhaps an inevitable one—to the sharp decline in the value of acquisitions budgets. When funds become scarce, it is pragmatic and realistic to funnel them to specific needs and to allow academic staff to determine priorities and balances within the collection. Nevertheless, it means a major diminution of the role of academic librarians; responsibility for collection development ideally belongs with the library, not academics, and once given away it will be hard to recover. Allowing faculties to determine allocations for books and periodicals, and between subjects, is an abdication of the professional responsibilities of librarians.

Regaining control over collection development should be a major aim for many university libraries. But there are some aspects of collection building which are almost always librarians' responsibility and do not come within the scope of subject allocations for books and periodicals. Most libraries have special collections of some sort, created by donation or purchase. In the present financial climate, however, these collections cannot usually be added to by buying more material, except in the largest libraries. Maintaining their value for research in very specific areas now depends partly on further donations, and mainly on the quality of the original collection. Few libraries can afford to spare enough staff to manage these collections adequately. Whether they are books, archives, or manuscripts, such special collections have generally been another casualty of the drift toward emphasizing current needs, rather than assembling materials as the basis for future research. Outside the large research libraries, it is now rare to find special collections growing in size and staff, though Southampton is the exception.

Donations are another aspect of collection building for which librarians still have responsibility. At one extreme are the provisions for copyright deposit, affecting Cambridge and the Bodleian, that include the requirement to preserve British publications indefinitely and make them available for research. The volume of deposit material is now nearly 130,000 volumes a year; recent automation of the recording and claiming procedures of the Copyright Agency has helped to increase the amount of material being deposited. At the other extreme are the small, irregular gifts received by all libraries, usually with no conditions attached. In between are the more regular arrangements for donations, notably those for publications of the European Communities. Many university libraries are European Documentation Centres and receive a rapidly increasing amount of material in this way, resulting in substantial problems of space and access. All these gifts create problems of selection, housing, and access to some degree or another.

Another area of collection building which is usually the responsibility of librarians rather than academics is audiovisual material. For the majority of academics, library collections consist only of books and periodicals; if the library wants to build up an audiovisual collection, it must set aside special funds and expect to do most of the material selection. All libraries have collections of microforms, though these are often little more than back runs of newspapers and parliamentary documents. Many libraries keep their microforms in a separate area or room, but some divide them by subject and house them near the appropriate printed material. Substantial collections of other types of audiovisual material are uncommon, and are usually found in smaller, newer libraries like Exeter, Kent, City, and Sussex. These tend to emphasize one or two categories: slides, video and audio tapes, or records. Collections of computer software for loan are even more uncommon. Most audiovisual collections are in a separate room, usually comparatively hard to reach. The new library at Newcastle is unusual for having playing equipment as a standard feature on each floor. Because of the uncertain financial climate, audiovisual collections will be difficult to build up in the future unless a library can keep sufficient funds under its own control to allocate accordingly. With inadequate money for books and periodicals, expenditure on audiovisual materials will be hard to justify to unsympathetic academic staff.

With librarians abandoning much of their control over subject allocations and collection building, their main contribution to maximizing the value of the acquisitions budget may be limited to ensuring that the best possible terms are obtained from suppliers. Some libraries are now using automated acquisitions and accounting systems to assess the performance of suppliers and compare prices. But most libraries are not doing this, or only attempt it occasionally and informally. There is a strong tendency to prefer continuity and to maintain an existing pattern of supply. Most libraries use library suppliers rather than deal directly with publishers. Some follow a policy of using one or two British suppliers for most acquisitions, while others prefer to deal with suppliers in the country of origin. Many use the local university bookshop to buy some or most of their books. There is scope for much greater use of prepayment plans and for a more rigorous approach to comparing prices and discounts, as long as the university's financial practices are maintained. Consistency of supply and quality of service from suppliers have always been given high priority by university libraries, but the severe pressure on acquisitions budgets requires that these considerations be placed second to the actual cost.

The decline in funding has also affected libraries' ability to make adequate arrangements for the preservation and conservation of their collections. This is especially evident in a reduction of binding. Between 1981/82 and 1984/85, 56% of libraries cut down on the volume of material being bound, and 65% made greater use of "economy binding," principally plastic jackets like Lyfgards. In 1985/86, binding was reduced by 28% of libraries and economy binding increased in 37%.[10] In many cases, the changes were substantial. Some libraries now bind very little material at all, and quite a few follow a policy of buying paperbacks in preference to hardbacks and using Lyfgards. The smaller libraries, which do not have their own binderies, have cut or held static their budgets for commercial binding. Larger libraries with their own binderies have allowed staff to run down and have endeavoured to raise their income from commercial work outside the library.

These changes in binding have become part of the major and urgent problem of preserving library collections. The national scale of this problem was identified in the Ratcliffe report of 1984, which also made recommendations for tackling the specific difficulties involved: the acid content of modern paper, the inadequacy of resources for training conservation techniques, and the uncertain archival life of new forms of library materials.[11] But only the largest research libraries are already devoting staff and funds to preservation; the other university libraries have no money to spare to cope with such newly identified and expensive problems. The importance of preservation to such libraries lies not so much in the conservation of antiquarian material, but in ensuring that current material in heavy use does not become so damaged as to be unusable. Even in this area, though, the sharp decline in the real value of library budgets is forcing most libraries to give no thought to the future. Current and immediate demands, in the narrowest sense, have come to dominate the maintenance of library collections, as well as their acquisition and selection.

REFERENCES

1. SCONUL. *Survey of funding cuts 1979/80–1984/85*; *Survey of funding 1984/85–1985/86*.

2. For the financial statistics in this chapter, I have drawn on: *University statistics, vol. 3, Finance*; and Arthur Davies, "A review of funding and its implications for collection development and access in university libraries," in : *Research collections under constraint and the future co-ordination of academic and national library provision* (London: SCONUL, 1986) (British Library R&D report 5907), pp. 7-29.

3. Index of University Costs for books, periodicals and binding in: SCONUL. *Annual report* 1986, p. 96. CLAIM/LISU indices in: *Average prices of British academic books*, and *Average prices of USA academic books* (in CLAIM report series). Blackwell periodicals index: published annually in the *Library Association Record*.

4. Survey by the Association of University Teachers (AUT), reported in the *Times Higher Education Supplement*, 12 February 1988.

5. SCONUL. *University library expenditure statistics*, 1981/82–

6. Statistics given in papers by Alan Singleton and Rebecca Lenzini at the 10th Conference of the U.K. Serials Group, Oxford, 1987 (forthcoming).

7. See note 4 above.

8. Pocklington, Keith. *Research collections under constraint* (London: British Library, 1987).

9. Peasgood, Adrian N. "Towards demand-led book acquisitions?" *Journal of librarianship* 18 (1986), pp. 242-256; Young, R.C. et al. "Geac with local enhancements: The integrated real-time system at the University of Sussex" *Program* 20 (1986), pp. 1-25.

10. SCONUL. *Survey of funding cuts 1979/80–1984/85; Survey of funding 1984/85–1985/86*.

11. Ratcliffe, F.W. *Preservation policies and conservation in British libraries* (London: British Library, 1984) (Library and information research reports; p. 25).

Chapter 5

Services and Buildings

University libraries have experienced much greater demand for their services. The changes in universities have created a more competitive and uncertain climate in which there is considerably more pressure on academic staff and students alike. Researchers are expected to produce good results more often and more quickly. Students are having to rely less on their teachers for detailed assistance, as staff numbers decline and staff/student ratios worsen, and as teaching methods place more emphasis on individual project work and assignments. In the near future, teachers are going to find the quality of their teaching being evaluated formally by the university. All these changes are encouraging or forcing staff and students to make greater and more demanding use of the library. Unfortunately for the library and for its users, this increased demand has come at a time when the real value of acquisitions budgets has been falling markedly, and when the number of posts in libraries has been reduced substantially. Libraries must therefore meet greater demands with fewer resources.

Most libraries have tried to avoid needing to choose between collections and services as the greater priority. But for many the continuing decline in acquisitions budgets makes this a losing battle; they are discovering that such a choice is necessary if mediocrity in both areas is to be resisted. A few of the smaller, technological university libraries have already made a conscious choice to give services a greater priority and to improve access to materials held elsewhere, rather than aim to build large local collections. The largest research libraries still have the resources to provide a library service based primarily on research materials of great breadth, exploited and made available by the scholarship of well-qualified staff. But, most libraries are somewhere between the two extremes. They run the risk of being unable to provide either good collections or good services, because financial cutbacks are making it increasingly unrealistic to aim for both.

The choice is further complicated by the structure of most library budgets, which separate staff from materials; the growing trend toward one-line, all-inclusive budgets where the librarian can set priorities many allow greater freedom of action. But better services almost inevitably mean more staff, and the universities are at present insisting on staff reductions and are even setting limits for staffing expenditure within one-line budgets. It is therefore difficult to plan for a higher and more intensive level of service to compensate for a decline in collection growth. The more realistic alternative is a change of direction for services, so that greater emphasis is placed on access to resources and information held outside the library, on promotion of the library's services, and on tailoring them to the needs of specific users. In almost all libraries this would have to be done with the same or fewer staff, and would mean a major shift in the emphasis of their work. Some libraries are already making such a shift; others, even when they have a team of subject specialists, still give greater emphasis to the development and exploitation of the library's own collections. But with the general decline in the real value of library budgets, this can only result in a worsening level of service based on an increasingly inadequate collection.

This growing inadequacy of services can be seen most generally in reduced operating hours of libraries. Between 1979/80 and 1984/85, 55% of libraries responding to the SCONUL survey reduced their opening hours. A further 7.5% reduced their hours in 1985/86.[1] Most of these reductions were in weekend hours, in the evening, and outside university terms. The opening times of branch libraries also were often reduced. Nevertheless, most libraries still open during the weekend and in the evenings during term-time. At least two libraries open half an hour later, one day a week, to provide time for staff training. More significant than these reductions in operating hours, however, has been the increasing tendency to close down specific service desks. This has meant that specialized service points, like audiovisual rooms, periodicals enquiry desks, or special collections may open later in the morning, close for lunch, or close earlier in the evenings than the rest of the library. More general services have also been affected, with many libraries being unable to staff enquiry desks between 9 a.m. and 5 p.m., or even closing issue desks at lunchtime. Quite a few libraries have had to resort to opening in the evenings and on weekends without any services. The library then functions as no more than a large reading-room, with only a minimal staff to ensure a basic level of security. No books are issued and no enquiries are answered. This type of opening without services is mainly of benefit to undergraduates, at least in Aston's experience. But even for them the absence of the on-line catalogue and of photocopying facilities was seen as a major disadvantage.

Reduction of operating hours and times when particular services are available can be extremely irritating to library users. Students and academic staff are both likely to resist such reductions and to press for increased hours. Aston's Sunday opening without services was in response to repeated requests from students; at Oxford, a proposal to reduce hours in the Bodleian and close some reading rooms was strongly opposed and eventually defeated by the university. The factors contributing to the increasing level of demand in university libraries are also leading students and academics to require greater availability of the library in the most general sense — the amount of time it is open. Part-time students, for whom evening and weekend services are vital, are growing in number and will become more important in the university and in government projections of student numbers. It is therefore essential for libraries to give a high priority to halting and even reversing the trend to shorter hours. Because current staffing levels are inadequate for providing a full range of services whenever the library is open, more libraries will have to resort to opening without services, employing special evening and weekend staff, and being more selective in staffing specialized service points. The specific inconveniences these measures undoubtedly cause are still preferable to the more general failure of closing the library altogether if services cannot be provided.

The services which university libraries provide are still largely based on the idea that the library should wait for users to come forward with enquiries and demands, rather than aim to anticipate and increase such demands by promoting its services to individual users. To a considerable extent this is still justified, since many researchers and academic staff feel it is for *them* to determine the timing and extent of the library's involvement in their research. What most libraries have tried to do, in the face of such attitudes and within the limitations imposed by staff shortages and inherited patterns of staffing and services, is to increase the range of services available, devote a greater proportion of staff to them, and endeavour to increase awareness. Only a few libraries have tried to develop their services believing that a higher priority should be given to anticipation of demand, and promotion and tailoring of services. Even these libraries are still faced with the fact that their collections, with the associated catalogues and issue systems, impose, by their very existence, a less active role for academics and researchers.

Most libraries have put increasing effort into instructing their readers (primarily students) to make use of the library. Tape-slide programmes or videorecordings are often used to introduce new users to the library. Some libraries give introductory tours, while others rely on self-guided tours. A few take a more active approach by teaching courses or seminars on library use to specific groups of students, though this has sometimes been a casualty of academic or library staffing cuts, as at Surrey. Some libraries have suitable accommodations available for teaching; permanent teaching rooms equipped with videorecorders, computer terminals, or overhead projectors are increasingly common. This type of user education is especially associated with the technological university libraries, and is intended to give students some idea of the structure of publishing and sources of information in particular subjects. Models of research methods in these subjects tend to be presented in a simplified way. There is also a strong tendency to reduce this instruction to an account of the reference materials in the library, and of how to make use of the library in a fairly narrow, functional sense.

Most libraries produce many leaflets and printed guides. These are usually devoted to a particular topic, such as the catalogues or inter-library loans, or to particular sections of the library's collections—either subjects or special collections and materials. They often also include plans of the shelf arrangement. Many libraries have an extensive range of these leaflets, and quite a few have made an effort to standardize the format and appearance of guides, which may be produced by several different departments within the library. Without such standardization and attention to the quality of presentation, library guides and leaflets tend to look amateurish and uninteresting. Perhaps because of the cost of producing them or because of staff shortages, a few libraries fail to keep their leaflets up to date or run out of stock, which adds to the amateurish effect. The proliferation of guides and leaflets is likely to be as much of a deterrent as a help to users of the library, especially when all the leaflets are displayed in a single large rack, as is often the case. The amount of material and of detail is something of an admission that university libraries are not sufficiently self-explanatory for finding one's way to the basic services.

More importantly, perhaps, these leaflets and guides usually mirror the functional and subject structure of the library. In other words, they explain how the library is organized and what its different sections do, rather than describing what the library can offer to particular types of users. There are exceptions to this; Newcastle, for example, limits its leaflets to a series designed for university staff, students, postgraduates, and external borrowers. Each leaflet gives a brief account of the services of most interest to that group of users, with information on opening hours and staff members to contact. The leaflet for university staff, in particular, contains sections titled "How the library can support your teaching" and "How the library can support your research."

Durham and York produce similar guides within a wider, functionally based set. This type of leaflet is valuable because it tries to see the library from the user's point of view. Too little use is also made of displays and exhibitions in this context. A decreasing number of libraries, but still probably a majority, have space set aside for such purposes, but it is almost always used to exhibit special collections and rare material, or for commemorations and external exhibitions. None of these helps to promote the library's services directly. There is considerable scope instead for an active and interesting programme of displays which explain and highlight the ways in which the library can be of service to particular users.

The nature of the potential user population is beginning to change. For most libraries, the majority of their users are undergraduate students who traditionally have been full-time, between the ages of 18 and 25, and living close to the campus. Universities are already making an effort to increase the number of overseas students, mainly because of the fees they pay, and this has important implications for libraries. In general, overseas students place a disproportionately greater burden on the library in that they need and expect a much higher level of assistance from staff than British students do, and they have difficulty understanding instructions if their command of English is weak. They usually spend more time in the library than English-speaking students, especially on weekends. In the future more overseas students are expected, and libraries must be prepared to provide services and assistance at a level appropriate for them. Otherwise, potential students from overseas will be discouraged from coming to a particular university, and the library will find itself taking the blame for the university's loss of revenue.

There will also be more part-time and mature-entry students than has been usual in the past. They too have different needs and expectations when using the library. Part-time students need satisfactory hours and services outside the normal working day. The time they have for using the library is limited; when particular items or services are unavailable during that time, hardship is incurred. Mature-entry students appear, as a general rule, to be much more committed and highly motivated than the typical full-time student. They too are likely to expect a higher standard of service from the library, and to be more impatient with inadequacies. They may also require more help with the basic library services if they have not used similar libraries in recent years. These mature-entry, part-time, and overseas students are all likely to comprise an increasingly large proportion of library users in the future, and libraries must be prepared for the different demands they will bring.

For undergraduates, most libraries offer a fairly limited range of services, with the emphasis on the circulation system, the short loan collection, and photocopying. Access to more specialized services like inter-library loans and on-line searching is restricted to final-year undergraduates at best, and subject services are largely limited to assistance in finding and using the relevant section of the shelves. Most libraries concentrate on ensuring that items on reading-lists are readily available in multiple copies, usually with restricted loan periods and as long as funds permit. This may not be enough to satisfy the newer types of students already mentioned. Libraries are also coming under pressure from the growing tendency to expect undergraduates to undertake projects and assignments in which they are forced to find relevant material for themselves, instead of being given a reading-list. Such projects demand more specialized help and services than are usually available to undergraduates. Conflicting attitudes among academic staff may add to these difficulties; some may encourage their students to ask for help from subject librarians, while others may regard such help as undermining the initiative they are expecting their students to show. Librarians cannot ignore such changes in teaching methods, if they hope to make library services relevant to undergraduates.

At a more general level, the tendency to base services and acquisitions on undergraduate reading-lists, in conjunction with limiting collections to material needed for current research, makes the library *less* valuable for undergraduates. One of the most important services university libraries have performed for suitably motivated undergraduates has been to enable them to educate themselves by going beyond the structure of courses and reading-lists to investigate other subjects and other intellectual approaches. This does not require a large research collection, but it does require a well-rounded and broadly based collection which is not limited to current reading-lists and research. A few libraries have tried to use so-called "leisure collections" to meet this need for a broader selection of material, but these are essentially popular novels or books on recreational activities, not a contribution to a university education in the true sense. The ability of libraries to contribute to the self-education and intellectual development of undergraduates has been, probably unintentionally, a service of great value, and should not be allowed to wither away as the result of an exclusive emphasis on meeting current teaching needs.

Services to research students and academic staff are more specialized, more active, and better promoted than those for undergraduates. A system of subject librarians often provides the basic framework for these services, with a strong emphasis on regular liaison with particular departments or schools. This should, in theory, allow for the very different requirements of users in different subject areas.

Research methods differ considerably between disciplines, and so do means of communicating new research findings. The extent to which researchers rely on the written record of previous research also varies in different disciplines. University libraries, which provide access to that record, are therefore less central to research in some subjects, and have a varying place in the research process. A researcher who is editing a literary or historical text has very different library requirements from those of a member of a research team working on practical applications of the latest work in electronics or medicine. These different requirements are evident in most universities, though the specialized schools and technological universities are much less affected.

Despite the prevalence of subject specialists, libraries take little notice of these major differences. All subject librarians tend to offer the same basic mix of services, with varying emphases for different subjects: help in using the collections, either by instruction or by answering specific enquiries; on-line searching; so-called "literature searches" in printed abstracting and indexing journals; and passing on information about developments in the field from such sources as publishers' blurbs and advertisements for conferences, new products, and the like. Even with all these activities, much of the subject librarians' time is taken up with maintaining, and to a lesser extent developing, the library's collections in their subject area. While these services are undoubtedly useful to academic staff and researchers, they do not do enough to convince such users that the library is an essential part of their work. In an age when much information is available on-line and when most university libraries have increasingly narrow collections, this half-heartedness is not enough. Researchers will either make more use of direct on-line access themselves or go in person to the largest research libraries, depending on their field of study. The local university library will become peripheral to their research.

Convincing researchers that the library is essential to their research involves a change in presentation and attitude, more than a change in the range of services. There is always a need for librarians to ensure that new services—like providing information from compact discs or access to computer networks and electronic mail—are added to those already in the library's repertoire. Another important line of development lies in providing more information about university activities, such as the database of theses and dissertations compiled at Bradford. But expanding the range of services available is only valuable when those services are presented properly to researchers. Too many libraries try to offer the same mix of services to all academic, or announce that such services are available and wait for interested users to make contact with library staff. Proper presentation involves first of all understanding in some depth the different methods and subjects relevant to individual researchers, along the lines suggested by Brenda Moon in a recent article.[2] Then the available services can be selected and tailored to fit their different needs in a more deliberate and sophisticated way.

This kind of promotion is more difficult in larger libraries which serve universities with a large number of academic staff doing a wide variety of research. These libraries' efforts are bound to be more superficial and directed at groups rather than individuals. But unless their collections are among the few which are still largely self-sufficient for research, their efforts also run the risk of becoming peripheral and irrelevant to academic researchers. Their aim should still be "services to research" (rather than "information services" or "reference services") if they want to lessen this risk. Smaller libraries with a more restricted group of researchers to serve are finding it easier to change to a type of service more closely targeted to specific individuals. Libraries like Aston and Salford are following this path already, but their strong emphasis on technological subjects and on-line methods reflects the bias of their universities, and is not a characteristic necessary to promote library services. The general attitude is what matters, with a determination to make the library an essential part of university research.

A considerable incentive for tailoring library services will come from changes in university budgeting. As more universities give their departments or schools a one-line budget with freedom to decide how to spend their allocation, more academics will consider using some of their funds for library purposes. This has already happened at a few institutions, such as UWIST, where departments have financed staff and materials for special services particularly relevant to them, like a Company Information Service and a Technical Reference Bureau for architecture. There are other, more ominous, signs of departments reconsidering the usefulness of the library: suggestions that money for library acquisitions should come from departmental allocations instead of a central library fund; controversies surrounding the division of library materials budgets among subjects; and changes to the scope of such budgets to include on-line searching and inter-library loans. The major changes to resource allocation and financial control which are taking place in all universities are helping to create a climate where the library must be perceived as essential to research. If it is seen as peripheral and irrelevant in its present form, the pressures to reduce its financial independence will grow.

In this context, the pursuit of more external, non-university users seems to be a dead end. The largest research libraries inevitably attract external and international users because of the unique value of their collections. Some other libraries are obliged to provide access for professional groups like doctors and teachers as part of the conditions attached to the founding or endowment of a separate medical or education library. Quite a few libraries are keen to encourage other individual or corporate users as a means of raising extra money in financially difficult times. But such users can only be a distraction if the library's efforts are directed to specific research needs of university staff. Special services for external users should ideally be a university activity undertaken in the library, rather than an independent initiative by the library. Warwick's Business Information Service, for example, is associated with the library but administered directly by the university; it has its own staff and its profits go to the university rather than the library. Tenants of university science parks are an ambiguous case, being closely linked to the university but not part of it. The services they require are likely to be commercial and industrial rather than academic, and may not complement the kinds of services provided for university researchers. The main criterion for offering services to external users should usually be the university's own attitude. If such services can be provided as an integral part of the university's external fund-raising, the library will be helping to strengthen its value to the university.

While all libraries make an effort to communicate with their different types of users, comparatively few have formal channels through which the users themselves can initiate communication with the library. The changes in university organizational structures are making it even less likely than before that the Library Committee will include this among its functions. Separate user groups, liaison committees, and student committees exist in some universities and provide another avenue of communication which will be more frequently used in the future. Faculty Library Committees, where these exist, are accountable to the faculty rather than the library; membership of academics and library staff is not usually on equal footing. The matters raised by library users in these various committees tend to concern either broad library policy or the details of library operations. There is untapped potential for using such committees as one way of reaching agreement on services tailored to specific users. Another avenue of communication from users is the suggestion book or suggestion board, but only a minority of libraries use these. These too concentrate on details of library operations, and can easily descend to a forum for vulgarity or abuse; it is unusual to find the chief librarian answering suggestions personally.

Within the library, most enquiries from users are aimed at a small enquiry desk close to the main entrance. In a few libraries this desk is not immediately obvious upon entering the library, but in most it is meant to be clearly visible from the entrance. The desk is usually staffed by a professionally qualified librarian, but not necessarily one of the academic-related staff. Some libraries roster such staff for duty at the enquiry desk, while others appoint one or two as its permanent staff. A few libraries cannot staff their enquiry desk continually during the day, and at least one has made a decision to withdraw staff from this desk and leave it as a self-service information point with leaflets and a telephone. The basic function of a general enquiry desk is to filter questions from users, directing them to a more appropriate source if necessary. A substantial number of libraries have enquiry desks on their subject floors too, to deal with more specialized requests for assistance or information. These are rarely staffed for the whole of the normal working day. Subject specialists frequently have an office or other accommodation behind the scenes, either on the entrance floor or the subject floors, and are not necessarily based at a subject enquiry desk.

A few libraries offer television Videotex services linked to their general enquiry desk, with access to the brief and factual information broadcast on the CEEFAX and ORACLE services, and sometimes to the PRESTEL Viewdata service as well. In most cases, the staff of the enquiry desk keep the control pad for the television set, and library users must ask to use it. At Hull, similar equipment not far from the enquiry desk is used for the university's electronic bulletin-board service.

It is too early to assess trends in the volume of work handled by enquiry desks until SCONUL's statistics cover a greater period.[3] But there is clear evidence that demand for lending services has increased, despite falls in the numbers of students and academic staff. At City University, heavily cut in 1981, loans rose by about 35% between 1980/81 and 1985/86, even with a temporary reduction of 10% in 1983/84. Loans from the main library at Swansea rose nearly 21% between 1980/81 and 1985/86, compared with a rise in student numbers of 11%. At Hull during the same period, loans from the main library rose nearly 9% while the number of academic and student readers fell by more than 11%. Cambridge, with its very different user population and lending policies, experienced a rise of 20% in loans between 1983/84 and 1985/86. Coping with increases like these with a smaller staff has forced a few libraries to lengthen their normal loan periods in order to reduce the frequency of circulation. Others have introduced or improved automated issue systems to meet a greater demand with fewer staff.

A substantial number of libraries allow users to have on-line access to data about circulation, either through an on-line public access catalogue or, more usually, through terminals linked to the issue system. The information provided usually covers whether an item is on loan, details held on the system about the borrower, and a list of the borrower's loans. Reservations are rarely available on-line. Some libraries are willing to disclose the current borrower of an item, and are now obliged to conform to the provisions of the Data Protection Act if they make such disclosures. Most libraries fine at least some categories of users for some breaches of borrowing regulations, especially in connection with short loan collections. Most libraries now have such collections of reading-list material in heavy demand from students; some supplement them with special shorter loan periods for similar material on the open shelves. Most short loan collections are on closed access, though a few are open to readers to browse and sometimes even to work in. Libraries with microfiche catalogues find it difficult to mark which items are in the short loan collection, and are usually forced to provide a separate list printed out from the circulation system. St Andrews provides an on-line booking system for its collection.

There is considerable variation in the type of catalogues provided. Most libraries have a current catalogue on microfiche, though some now have an on-line catalogue available. A few libraries still use cards or sheaf. Many libraries still have a separate catalogue for their periodicals in the form of either a special computer printout, a separate sequence of microfiche or cards, or a separate file in the on-line catalogue (as at Cambridge). The dominant form of access in microfiche and card catalogues is still the classified sequence, with a separate sequence for names and titles, and an alphabetical subject index for the classification scheme. Most, but not all, libraries with a classified catalogue provide such an index on microfiche, computer printout, cards, or even a visible index. Several of the London libraries provide microfiche catalogues with sequences for names and titles, classification, and Library of Congress subject headings. But catalogues limited to names, titles, and alphabetical subject headings are rare. Reading has a single-sequence microfiche catalogue covering these access points; Swansea has a divided catalogue of the same scope. Sheffield also has a divided microfiche catalogue of this type, inputting Library of Congress subject headings as local data rather than accepting BLCMP's (Birmingham Libraries Co-operative Mechanization Project) standard classified catalogue.

The on-line public access catalogues (OPACs) are divided into two types: those linked to an automated cataloguing system, and those linked to an automated circulation system. Quite a few libraries which are not yet in a position to offer the first type of OPAC have made the second type available as a substitute. The access points in this type depend on the software involved, though none is very sophisticated. London University's EUCLID, linked to its Geac circulation system, can be accessed by author, title, ISBN, or Library of Congress card number; SWALCAP's (South Western Academic Libraries Co-operative Automation Project) circulation system can be accessed by author, title, or classmark, as at UWIST, Aberystwyth, and Swansea. Other libraries (like Hull, Lancaster, and Manchester) have written or adapted software to give more flexible access to circulation files, including by keywords.

The "genuine" OPACs based on automated cataloguing systems are quickly becoming more common, though still very much a minority. Some are commercial systems from a range of suppliers but predominantly Geac, while others have been written specially for the library concerned. Both types of OPAC do not vary greatly in their methods of searching. The CLSI system at Heriot-Watt offers author, title, and classmark searches, while Geac offers author and/ or title, names as subjects, classmark, and keyword in most of its installations. Edinburgh also has searching on Library of Congress subject headings. The other commercial systems and the in-house systems usually provide similar types of searches, with classification being more common than subject headings and the two rarely being found together. Cambridge offers a combined keyword search on author, title, and subject headings. Dobis-Libis at Liverpool provides a search by publisher. A few of the OPACs provide Boolean searching, but hardly any allow further refinement of searches by publication date, language, type of material, and so on; Newcastle's OCLC (Online Computer Library Center) system is the most sophisticated in this respect. Almost all OPACs provide circulation information about individual items, though few allow readers to place their own reservations.

Though these OPACs undoubtedly provide much more flexible access to authors, titles, and other names, they do little, on the whole, to improve subject access. Classmark searches are hardly used at all, according to Sussex's transaction logs of searches,[4] yet they are often the only method of subject access apart from title keywords. Searches on Library of Congress subject headings, even when they are available, are inherently difficult to use successfully without keyword access. Browsing on classmarks is not often available as a direct link from the results of a keyword search, though BLCMPs OPAC and the circulation-based in-house systems at St Andrews and Manchester provide for this. A few OPACs also offer files of information about the library: operating hours, staff details, other services, recent accessions, and even current exhibitions. Floor plans of the library are not yet available on-line, though one or two libraries are working on this. Hull provides access to some university information, including a list of vacancies from the Careers Office, as well as access to electronic mail. York is unique in offering access to five other OPACs as part of its standard menu, through the Joint Academic Network (JANET).

Most libraries have two or more catalogues. The older catalogue is usually on cards, but sometimes has been microfiched and has usually been closed to new entries. Only a few libraries can claim that more than 80% of their stock is covered by a single on-line system, but many are working on retrospective conversion of older titles. Several of these conversions are long-term and large-scale; many have used temporary staff supplied under a grant from the Manpower Services Commission, though a few libraries have used commercial bureaux.[5] For retrospective conversions and current cataloguing alike, libraries are using a range of external sources for bibliographic records: BLCMP, SWALCAP, OCLC, BLAISE (British Library Automated Information Service), REMARC (Retrospective Machine-readable cataloguing), and the Cambridge database. Quite a few libraries still create catalogue records themselves. A substantial number of on-line catalogues, especially those derived from circulation data, contain minimal-level records, while most commercial OPACs allow more than one level of record display based on a fairly full record. The Cambridge OPAC offers a format setting which allows the user to choose a standard display ranging from a one-line summary to an on-line catalogue card. Control of standards and consistency depends entirely on the type of catalogue used and the source of records, and varies considerably.

As far as inter-library loans are concerned, most libraries have been trying to reduce a level of demand which has tended to rise dramatically if unchecked. There is usually a separate budget for this service, which imposes a ceiling on the number of loans. As local collections become more inadequate with the decline in the real value of acquisitions budgets, there is inevitably an increased demand for inter-library loans, which has reached the limit of funds. Between 1979/80 and 1984/85, 40% of libraries had to take measures to discourage requests for inter-library loans, and a further 19% did so in 1985/86.[6] The usual method has been to impose a limit on the number of items which can be requested by one person in a given period. Many libraries now do this: Hull and Bradford set daily limits, Brunel and Kent have yearly limits, and Loughborough has both. Some libraries place a ceiling on the number of requests which can be in process: four at Manchester, five at Sussex, six at Swansea, and so on. Almost all libraries restrict this service to academics and postgraduates; some even require an academic's signature on a postgraduate's request. Some libraries charge the net costs of requests above these limits, while others make a token charge of 50 pence or less to discourage unnecessary requests. Brunel and Aberystwyth charge for photocopies received on inter-library loan, while Southampton introduced such a charge but was forced to withdraw it after opposition from users.

The British Library's Document Supply Centre is the source for most inter-library loans, with regional lending bureaux playing a minor role. As a result, most libraries have to draw directly on their budget for nearly all the material they request. A few libraries like Bath, Edinburgh, and UWIST include inter-library loans in a general allocation to faculties or departments. It is then possible for academics to decide the appropriate balance between borrowing material from another library and buying it for retention in the local library. This avoids forcing the library to set limits on such borrowing or to charge for it, which are unfortunate and unwelcome developments at a time when access to library services is becoming more important than building a local collection. But it allows academics to have control over what should be a professional decision for librarians, and limits even further inter-library borrowing of academic staff, rather than of postgraduates or even undergraduates. The increased demand for inter-library loans is not simply the result of periodical cancellations.[7] It is an integral part of changes in research methods and information needs, as well as a consequence of less adequate local collections. Borrowing such material ought to be treated as one avenue through which the library can meet the demands of individual researchers, instead of as a separate, additional service. But the decision to use inter-library borrowing should be the responsibility of specialist library staff with a good understanding of researchers' requirements.

On-line searching is in general still treated as a separate, additional service. In many libraries, such searches are conducted in a special room using special equipment. Providing subject librarians with their own personal computers on their desks or in their offices has rarely been adopted as a standard pattern, though Bath is one example. There is a general drift away from the idea that one or two members of staff should specialize in on-line searching, and quite a few libraries are training a greater number of staff to carry it out. Many libraries impose some form of charge for this service: either the net cost of each search or a flat rate, with extra charges for printing more than a certain number of references. Several libraries subsidize the cost when charges are of the first type. Among the variations of the second type of charging is Lancaster's, where searches are free if the database is not held by the library in printed form, and £10 if it is; printing more than 25 references costs 10-15p per reference in either case. Aberdeen charges a basic fee of £5 for up to five minutes and 25 references, with additional fees for more than this; a search lasting more than 30 minutes or producing more than 100 references is charged at full cost-recovery rates. These charges undoubtedly discourage researchers from using this service. Both Salford and Sussex recently stopped charging and experienced an immediate sharp rise in demand.

Even where on-line searching is provided free to users, most libraries are limited by the separate budget they have available. Including on-line searching in the allocation to faculties or departments is a solution that has been adopted at UWIST, King's College London, and Edinburgh, among others. The restriction of a separate budget is avoided, but the library loses control over determining appropriate services for particular needs. At Salford, the use of on-line searches depends on the professional judgement of the subject specialists; if they think a search is appropriate, it is free, but a user who insists on a search that a librarian thinks is inappropriate is obliged to pay. This type of integration of on-line searching into a package of available services, to be employed at the discretion of library staff, is an essential goal within a wider aim of making library services essential to researchers. As with inter-library loans, this depends heavily on integrated budgetary arrangements.

One service which has never created a financial problem is photocopying. In those libraries with some form of staffed service it usually pays for itself, while those with entirely unstaffed machines make a considerable profit. A growing number of libraries have introduced payment by cards rather than coins, which makes self-service photocopying much easier and raises use levels even further. With appropriate software, it will soon enable some analysis of photocopying by categories of user. Photocopying is one of the most important services provided by a library to its undergraduate users. But there is now the threat of problems regarding copyright. The government is now preparing new copyright legislation, while some publishers are trying to build an extra charge for photocopying into their charges to libraries for periodicals. The Copyright Licensing Agency and the universities have agreed on a blanket licensing scheme to pay for multiple copying in universities. It is not clear how such a scheme will affect libraries, which do not make multiple copies themselves, but at worst it might force them to monitor all photocopying by their users. Oxford and Cambridge have always done this as part of their responsibilities under copyright deposit, but it is rare for other libraries to require users to complete forms for all copying. Bath and Leeds do, however. Having to monitor all photocopying would considerably reduce libraries' income from this service, and would increase the inconvenience to users.

All these services, from photocopying to enquiry desks, depend considerably for their effectiveness on the building in which they are housed. Most university libraries (or at least their main sites) are now located in buildings which have been constructed or extended in the last 20 years. Despite the pressure on recurrent funds in the recent past, capital funds have been made available for new buildings at several libraries, notably Newcastle, Loughborough, and Exeter, and extensions to quite a few, including Aberdeen, Durham, Glasgow, Reading, and Southampton. Further extensions are just beginning or about to start, and a new library has been approved for Dundee. This building programme is in large part a consequence of the UGCs 1976 report on *Capital Provision for University Libraries*, better known as the Atkinson Report.[8] This set out new norms for library space requirements, which have been followed by the UGC ever since. The policy has been that a new building or extension is only justified if the area required under these norms is significantly greater than what is already available. The basic norm was calculated at 1.25 square metres per full-time-equivalent student—half is for shelving, one-third for seating, and the rest for administration. While this has enabled many libraries to build extensions or new buildings, it is now also being used to reduce space in a few cases. Hull and Edinburgh have considerably more space than what is suggested by the UGC norms, and they are having to give up parts of their main library buildings to other university uses.

The other side of the Atkinson Report was its insistence on greater systematic withdrawal of stock from libraries as part of the formula for calculating space requirements. This advocacy of the so-called "self-renewing library" aroused violent opposition at the time, for it seemed to imply a comparatively low ceiling for the size of university libraries. In the first place, it relegated material to closed-access reserve storage of a size sufficient to contain five years' accessions at current rates. If the total stock overflowed this storage and the norms for shelving space, surplus material would have to be disposed of and could not be used as an argument for more space. This point has not yet been reached by university libraries. Over 20 have reserve stores, often in the form of compact shelving: a few, like Exeter and Aberdeen, have been able to store material in an older library building vacated after an extension in a new main library. But there is yet very little systematic weeding of collections and relegating material to stores. Many libraries, though by no means all, are having increased difficulty finding space for their collections, services, and readers, and it appears likely that the level anticipated in the Atkinson Report will be reached by many in the next few years. As Michael Smethurst has pointed out, the application of the Atkinson norms to all libraries will need to be re-examined before then; if selectivity and rationalization in the universities as a whole are going to flow on to university libraries, there will have to be different measures of space requirements for those libraries acting as centres of excellence for the whole system.[9]

Most library buildings now fall into two main classes: the older group have large reading rooms with separate stack areas, while the newer and more common group are open-plan with mixed shelving and seating. A few libraries have an original building of one type and an extension of the other. Extensions in general have only served to complicate the layout of buildings rather than simplify them, leaving most like labyrinths with their many staircases and varying floor levels. Within the newer buildings certain trends can be observed. There is increased concern with preventing heat loss through small window and wall areas, and an increased use of full air-conditioning for the benefit of users and to provide suitable conditions for the preservation of materials. A growing interest in minimizing unnecessary lighting is reflected in Reading's use of automatic timer switches which give about five minutes' lighting in the stacks when a reader touches them; Southampton has installed electronic "presence detectors" which switch on lights in the stacks automatically when someone walks past them. There is also an emphasis on good provision for wiring for computer and audiovisual applications. The current fire regulations have tended to require heavy fire doors and enclosed staircases.

The new buildings have stressed above all flexibility and adaptability and have usually tried to avoid embodying the library's current organizational structure in the building itself. Staff areas are usually open-plan, and public access to staff is at counters rather than desks. Seating for readers includes a greater variety of types and sizes within one library to suit varied preferences, and enclosed study rooms for special categories of students are usually provided. There are almost always lifts as well as stairs. Considerable trouble is taken with signs; they are usually quite large and prominent, with white lettering on a coloured background as the norm. Sometimes signs are colour-coded to distinguish between floors, as at Reading, or between services and subjects, as at Glasgow. Floor plans are often available, but these vary in type and are generally low quality.

The main open-access collections are normally arranged in the same order as the classification scheme, though some libraries have chosen, or have been forced, to break up this order so as to provide a more logical grouping of subjects on each floor. Most libraries use either Dewey decimal or Library of Congress classifications; a few use UDC, a couple use Bliss, and some use homemade schemes. All have problems with inconsistency and suitability, usually compounded by the various prefixes and suffixes added to make the shelf-mark. Most libraries have difficulties providing rapid and accurate re-shelving of material; a few ask readers to re-shelve books themselves. Most libraries try to minimize distinctions by size in the way materials are shelved, though a few use several size categories which always make material more difficult for users to find.

Treatment of periodicals varies: a few libraries shelve them together with books for each narrow subject group, but most have a separate sequence for periodicals on each floor, or occasionally a floor for all the library's periodicals. These are quite often in alphabetical rather than classified order. Current issues are sometimes displayed in a special area on each floor and sometimes in one area for the whole library; quite a few libraries use sloped shelving for this display, while others use various types of flat shelving which is generally much less appealing.

Shelving for books and non-current periodicals vary greatly; the best have attractive wooden ends for each stack, while the worst consist entirely of metal and look cheap and tatty. In some libraries the colour of the shelving is either too dark or too obtrusive. The general preference in colour-schemes is for light brown, grey, and cream, though most libraries have some areas which are much less muted. A few are brighter throughout, occasionally rather obtrusively. Walls are frequently unpainted brick, or sometimes unpainted concrete.

Noise levels are a problem in many libraries. Some put up notices reminding readers of the need for silence, and others try to reduce the problem by carefully arranged seating and shelving. A few designate certain areas of the subject floors as places where silence must be observed and allow quiet conversation elsewhere; Brunel calls these areas its "silent zones."

Even more of a problem than noise is security. All libraries have had some experience of theft, whether of valuable books by professional thieves or of material on student reading-lists. A few, like Reading, have successfully prosecuted the culprits in court. To guard against thieves, most libraries rely on an automatic security system which uses sensitized magnetic strips inserted in the spine of a volume. Many do not use any other form of security check, even though such systems can be bypassed. Few libraries check all readers entering the building. Some check everyone as they leave; these are usually libraries without an automatic system, which rely on porters and insist that bags be left in an external cloakroom. The most security-conscious libraries, such as those in London, require a membership card to be produced on entry, do not allow bags into the library, and also have a check at the exit. A growing number have an automatic security system as well as an exit check. Closed-circuit television is hardly ever used though Southampton has it in its reading rooms for manuscripts and special collections, and Manchester has it on emergency exit doors.

Mutilation of library material is a growing problem, which may well have been encouraged by the introduction of automatic security systems. Effective counter-measures are still being developed; the most promising approach targets specific subjects where mutilation is occurring, and publicizes the fact to students and academic staff working in that subject. Staff safety is also a growing concern, especially in the case of female staff working at night or on the weekend. Several libraries have responded by setting a minimum level of staffing at these times, and ensuring that a senior member of staff is rostered for duty with well-defined procedures to be followed if the safety of staff is threatened. At least one university offers a taxi service to its female staff working at night.

At their best, the new library buildings are flexible, well arranged, attractively furnished, and designed for security and energy conservation. The new library at Newcastle, opened in 1982, is a good example of all these qualities. But many of these new buildings, and their predecessors, do not reach these standards. Like large numbers of university buildings, these libraries are now in need of substantial repairs and refurbishing. Cracked and leaking roofs, worn furniture, peeling paint and threadbare carpets all abound. These maintenance problems are especially noticeable in libraries of the late 1960s and early 1970s, which were often built using construction methods of dubious quality. Many of these libraries fail to meet the goals now aimed for in new buildings. They tend to be unpleasantly hot, poorly laid out, fairly inflexible, and badly furnished. They suffer from low ceilings, small windows with little natural light, and the bleakness of bare concrete or bricks. The extent to which this affects their users is a matter for speculation, but the more inspiring setting provided by most of the much older library buildings is obviously lacking. Libraries built before the Second World War may be functionally unsatisfactory too, but at least they are more attractive. Today's university libraries have abandoned beauty to aim for a well-ordered functionality. But the ability of library staff to provide a high quality service can be obstructed by functional inadequacies of the buildings in which they work.

REFERENCES

1. SCONUL. *Survey of funding cuts 1979/80–1984/85; Survey of funding 1984/85–1985/86.*
2. Moon, Brenda E. "Co-operative networks and service to the scholar: University library resources for online research," *British journal of academic librarianship* 1 (1986), pp. 41-52.
3. SCONUL. *SCONUL statistical database part II: Library operations 1984/85.*
4. Young, R.C., and S.R. Lee, "The Geac-based OPAC at the University of Sussex Library," *Program* 20 (1986), pp. 138-150.
5. Hoare, Peter A., "Retrospective catalogue conversion in British university libraries," *British journal of academic librarianship* 1 (1986), p. 95-131.
6. SCONUL. *Survey of funding cuts 1979/80–1984/85; Survey of funding 1984/85–1985/86.*
7. Burch, Brian, and Arthur Davies, *Acquisitions and inter-library loans: A correlation?* (SCONUL document 87/35).
8. University Grants Committee. *Capital provision for university libraries: Report of a working party* (London: H.M.S.O., 1976).
9. Smethurst, J. Michael, "The Atkinson Report – 10 years on," in: *The world of books and information: Essays in honour of Lord Dainton*, edited by Maurice Line (London: British Library, 1987), pp. 159-171.

Chapter 6

Automation

The development of automation in British university libraries has continued, despite the marked limitation in other areas of activity, notably staffing and acquisitions. When surveyed by SCONUL, 79% of university libraries said that they had received additional money for equipment for automation between 1979/80 and 1984/85; 34% had been given extra funds for staff. In 1985/86, 34% of libraries received additional money for equipment, and 9% for staff. Some 55% considered they had been able to devote an adequate level of funding to equipment for automation up to 1984/85, while 42% felt funds for equipment were adequate in 1985/86.[1] There is evidence here that provision for library automation has been perceived as more satisfactory than for other areas of library activity, but these statistics conceal a whole range of difficulties, tensions, and uncertainties about the future.

Almost all university libraries now use some type of automated system for at least some of their internal operations, with Keele the only major exception. All have access to external automated systems, particularly the commercial databases available on-line from hosts like Dialog and Data-Star. Automation is now applied to all areas of library activity, though it is still far more common for circulation, cataloguing, and information retrieval than for other areas. And university libraries as a whole have such a variety of systems that they provide a history of library automation in its various phases. Commercial systems or in-house, integrated or separate, shared or stand-alone — all these are still in evidence.[2]

Quite a few libraries are still pursuing in-house development, begun in the early 1970s by the pioneers of automation-use like Lancaster, Newcastle, and Southampton. These systems are characterized by their lack of integration and their tendency to be written for a particular make of computer. Some still operate on a batch basis, though others have been upgraded to, or written as, on-line systems. They usually run on a university mainframe or a minicomputer shared by the library and the university administration. Unique local facilities are often available, either to the public or to library staff, and specialized staff in the library (or sometimes from the university's computing services) are responsible for maintaining the system software. Many of these in-house systems are now run alongside a commercial system in the same library, each for a separate area (or areas) of library activity. In these cases, the balance between in-house and commercial systems varies considerably from library to library.

At Southampton, for example, circulation and acquisitions are in-house, on-line systems which run on the library's own minicomputer; they have been upgraded from earlier batch versions. For cataloguing, the SWALCAP shared system is used, producing a microfiche catalogue. Development of an OPAC is likely to occur by loading records from SWALCAP on to the university's IBM mainframe and providing access to them as part of the local area network, using retrieval software like STATUS. Special software would need to be written to link this to the library's circulation system. East Anglia is another library with in-house circulation and acquisitions, but cataloguing from a shared system (in this case, BLCMP). St Andrews uses BLAISE-LOCAS to produce its microfiche catalogue, but also has its own circulation system running on two parallel processors, which offers such features as on-line reservations and on-line booking for the short loan collection. A periodicals list and acquisitions accounts are held on a Vax computer shared with the university administration. Newcastle still has local circulation and acquisitions systems, the former running on a library machine, the latter on the university's mainframe, but has used the OCLC local system since 1982 for its cataloguing and OPAC, with records derived from the OCLC shared system.

Closer to the original in-house systems are Lancaster, Loughborough, and York. Loughborough runs circulation, cataloguing, and periodicals financial control on its own minicomputer; microfiche catalogues are produced from this. At Lancaster, the circulation system runs, with batch updates, on a Honeywell machine shared with the university administration. Cards for the library's card catalogue are produced from the same machine. The in-house acquisitions package, which runs on the library's Itoh computer, prints draft catalogue entries, offers access by a requester's initials, and maintains an ISBN prefix file. The library has developed public access to its circulation data, allowing searches by author/title, classmark, ISBN, a subject index to the Bliss classification, and periodical titles. Access is made difficult by the use of abbreviations in corporate names and periodicals titles, and by only a single access point for each item in the author/title file. A further development is an inter-library loans system, which runs on an IBM personal computer and allows access by citation, requester, and request number.

York's circulation system is also a batch one, running on a machine shared with the university administration (in this case, a DEC-10). It is used to produce both a card catalogue and a microfiche catalogue and is also available through public access terminals. This on-line access is intended to complement, rather than supersede, the fixed access of the catalogues and so is limited to searches by stock number or keyword; the latter covers author, title, and classmark, with Boolean operators available. There are other unusual features available to the public: library operating hours; access to the on-line catalogues of Cambridge, Edinburgh, Hull, Leeds, and London; and the inclusion of inter-library loans with loans from stock as part of a borrower's details. Surrey's circulation-based public access terminals also feature searching only by keywords with Boolean operators, together with library news, access to the local area network, and a current awareness service in tourism and hospitality.

As these systems show, there is scope for more local variation and ingenuity than is possible with the standard packages sold by commercial companies. Nevertheless, there are several major drawbacks to in-house library systems. Above all, they need specialized staff to develop and maintain them. At a time when universities and their libraries are generally under great pressure to reduce senior staff, a substantial systems section requires a recurrent commitment in staff costs which is hard to justify in the face of the availability of integrated commercial systems. A further major weakness is that libraries are much more dependent on the staff and machines of the university's computing services. Several libraries with in-house systems have had difficulty getting adequate support from these services. At Kent, the Registry's Administrative Computing Unit failed to provide satisfactory programs to transfer the local circulation system to a new minicomputer, and it continued to run on an old and inadequate machine while new solutions were sought. A similar situation developed at St Andrews, where urgent upgrading of the in-house circulation system was delayed indefinitely because the Administrative and Library Computing Unit could not schedule enough time to write the appropriate software.

More generally, many libraries which use university mainframes for part of the library's operations are running into difficulties with the cycle of replacement for these machines. As they become due for replacement, a new make of machine is frequently chosen, usually incompatible with the previous one. Libraries are then faced with the need to re-write their systems to make them workable on the new mainframe. Sheffield, for example, re-wrote and improved the software for the Serials Union List for South Yorkshire when the university changed from an ICL to an IBM mainframe in 1986. Aberdeen, Brunel, and Oxford are among the libraries facing difficulties caused by replacements scheduled for the immediate future. Almost all libraries currently using their own systems or shared systems as their predominant form of automation have some type of application running on a university mainframe. Periodicals lists are undoubtedly the most common, though acquisitions, specialized databases, and even circulation are occasionally found. All these could possibly become redundant with the replacement of this mainframe by a different make of computer.

Almost all in-house automation is incompatible with other libraries' automation. The major exception is the work done at Cambridge. The Cambridge on-line catalogue offers searches by author and/or title, Library of Congress subject headings, and keyword for all these; periodicals can be searched for by title keyword or by a "fingerprint" acronym. Three display formats are available, and the user can also choose between menu-driven searching and command-driven searching. Records can be edited or created on-line.

Like the separate circulation system, it runs on a Perkin-Elmer machine but the software can easily be adapted to other machines and is available for distribution under licence. Because of this, other libraries like Kent are considering the Cambridge catalogue system for their own use, and some (such as Newcastle) are using the software to provide access to their on-line catalogues through local area networks. The Cambridge software also appears likely to be used for access to the proposed joint index to the on-line catalogues of the seven member libraries of CURL (the Consortium of University Research Libraries). But this widening use of the Cambridge software for on-line catalogues is exceptional; all the other in-house systems have remained limited to the library where they were developed.

Most of the libraries with such systems are now looking closely at the possibility of replacing them with commercial systems. Some have already decided to do this; Aberdeen is introducing the Dynix system to replace its own circulation and cataloguing systems. Others, like Loughborough and York, are in the process of drawing up specifications and considering tenders from suppliers of commercial systems. The remainder are still committed to the path of in-house development, whether by choice or by financial necessity. Cambridge, for example, is working on an acquisitions system to add to its cataloguing and circulation systems.

Some libraries have taken a commercial system as a basis and adapted it so extensively that it has become largely unrecognizable. Both Hull and Sussex took the Geac circulation module and modified it in this way, until they now have effectively their own local system. Hull offers its users on-line access to the circulation files by author, title, classmark, and keyword (including Boolean operators), as well as to borrower information, two university files, and electronic mail. Catalogue cards are produced from this system. At present, however, Hull is planning a commercial system which will automate cataloguing and acquisitions as well as circulation. Sussex, in contrast, has added cataloguing, acquisitions, and some serials control functions to its adaptation of the Geac circulation module. Borrower information is only available through circulation terminals rather than OPAC ones and Boolean searching is not offered, but the system produces a considerable amount of management information about usage within subject areas and about patterns of searching in the on-line catalogue. Manchester has also adapted an existing circulation system (in this case, the Dutch system Tobias), which now has on-line public access by author, title, keyword, or a follow-on browse by classmark; periodicals are searched for by title or acronym. Considerable library information is also available, and there is the possibility of using the four-colour screens to produce graphic displays of library floorplans. This adapted circulation system is combined with a separate in-house acquisitions system and a manually produced card catalogue. These few hybrid systems are also likely to be fewer in number in the future, mainly because of the staff needed for development and maintenance.

The number of shared systems is shrinking too. They belong essentially to the later 1970s and early 1980s, when they enabled university libraries to automate some of their procedures without developing in-house systems. A considerable number of libraries still use some form of shared system, though there has been an increasingly pronounced swing away from them in the past decade. One has already faded from view, at least as far as university libraries are concerned; SCOLCAP, the Scottish Libraries Co-operative Automation Project, no longer has any university library taking its cataloguing services. Another, the British Library's BLAISE-LOCAS, still has a few university libraries among its customers. London and St Andrews, for example, have their microfiche catalogues produced through LOCAS (Local Catalogue Service). But the British Library closed LOCAS in 1988 after 14 years' operation, and its existing customers will only be served until they have local systems capable of producing catalogues for them. Several university libraries have already stopped using LOCAS in recent years, and for those that remain there is now strong pressure to do the same. BLAISE-LINE and the BLAISE Selective Record Service will continue to be a source of catalogue records for some university libraries, either by direct downloading or through magnetic tapes for loading to local systems.

Of much greater significance, however, are the shared systems run by BLCMP and SWALCAP. BLCMP's shared cataloguing system produces microfiche catalogues for several university libraries, most of which also use the circulation system (CIRCO), running on a minicomputer within the individual library. A few also use the shared acquisitions and ordering system. SWALCAP's shared cataloguing system is used by rather more libraries, together with its local circulation system. Some, like Exeter, Swansea, and UWIST, have provided on-line public access to the circulation files by author, title, or classmark; Reading offers its users access by barcode number. SWALCAP's shared system includes only a rudimentary provision for acquisitions, and only a couple of libraries, like UWIST, have made use of it.

The prevailing trend in library automation is toward turnkey integrated systems, and this is clearly illustrated by the way in which both SWALCAP and BLCMP have been developing stand-alone integrated systems. Almost all of the university libraries currently using the shared systems are planning to install BLCMP's BLS or SWALCAP's LIBERTAS as soon as funds are available. Both systems offer (or will be developed to include) circulation, cataloguing, OPAC, acquisitions, and serials control. Both are also working to add inter-library loans to the range of services offered. BLCMP provides "electronic office" software for word processing, spreadsheets, electronic mail, and the like. Some of these BLCMP applications have already been implemented in university libraries, since the BLS circulation module is the same as the CIRCO system already used in BLCMP shared systems, and the BLS acquisitions module is functionally identical to that in the shared system. Warwick and Bradford have implemented the BLS OPAC, which offers searching by title, author and title, and classmark, together with a file of library information. LIBERTAS has not yet been installed in a university library. Both are certain to be working in many university libraries in the near future.

One of their unique features is a direct link to the BLCMP and SWALCAP databases as the source of bibliographic records. BLCMP's database is particularly large, with five million records from BNB, Library of Congress, and BLCMP members, as well as British Books in Print. This link is at the heart of the shared systems, and has been transferred to the new standalone systems. Other libraries, without such a link, are using a variety of sources for the bibliographic records which are the foundation of any integrated system. A few libraries, like Glasgow and Edinburgh, use BLAISE as their source (in both cases with a Geac system), but many create their records themselves, often in brief form rather than MARC (Machine-readable Cataloguing). Bath, for example, withdrew from the shared SWALCAP system and turned to URICA with locally created records. Aston uses BLCMP records with a Geac system. In general, though, the use of stand-alone automated cataloguing systems has been carried out independently from the BLCMP and SWALCAP shared systems. The emergence of BLS and LIBERTAS will change this considerably. Those libraries which do not use external records at present may have to look at this policy more carefully, in the light of continuing pressure on staffing costs and in the context of re-examination of the level of detail and quality desirable for OPAC records. Minimal catalogue records are characteristic of the majority of public access systems at the moment, but many of these are simply the result of circulation-based, rather than catalogue-based, systems. It is likely that OPACs in the future will have fuller records than at present, mainly from external sources.

A growing source of external records, in addition to BLAISE and the shared systems, has been OCLC. Some libraries, such as Newcastle, Essex, Bangor, and Strathclyde, are using the OCLC shared system for their current cataloguing; others, like Kent, Leeds, and Oxford, are using it for retrospective conversion. A few are also using OCLC's local stand-alone system. Oxford has used this for a pilot project in three faculty libraries, initially for building a catalogue and OPAC, followed by circulation. Newcastle uses the OPAC, but has retained its in-house circulation and acquisitions systems. Strictly speaking, the OCLC local system is not integrated, since its recently developed acquisitions and serials control systems run on linked microcomputers. Its OPAC offers searches by personal name, title, an author/title acronym, or single keyword, as well as by classmark, and a variety of subject headings and other types of name; the ability to narrow a search by date or language is also available. As yet, however, the stand-alone system has only a very small part of the British university library market, and the future for it and the more heavily used shared system is made uncertain for the next few years by the gradual introduction of fundamental changes to the design and services of OCLC's shared system.

The first, and still the most popular, of the commercial stand-alone systems is also not an integrated system. Since Hull and Sussex bought the Geac circulation system at the beginning of the 1980s, quite a few other university libraries have made the same choice, though without following Sussex into modifying the Geac system extensively in-house. Most have only implemented either circulation or cataloguing or both, reflecting their priorities in the original purchase. Aston is one exception, having now also implemented the acquisitions and serials control modules, and Dundee is another. Almost all these Geac libraries provide on-line access for users, sometimes through an OPAC but often through public enquiry terminals linked to the circulation system. Almost all have also made this access available through the local area network and hence through the Joint Academic Network (JANET). Access is usually by author, title, or classmark, though keywords, control numbers, and subject headings are occasionally added. The quality of Geac's circulation system was a major factor in its spread in university libraries, together with the lack of competition from other commercial systems in the recent past. Now, however, the lack of integration, especially between the circulation system and the MARC Record Management System, is seen as a drawback and a weakness in comparison with other systems, and the financial uncertainty affecting the parent company in Canada has made potential customers more cautious. The proliferation of other integrated library systems has given British university libraries a growing range of choices when looking for a new system, whatever their previous history of automation.

University libraries have turned to systems other than Geac. City and Heriot-Watt have both installed CLSI's Libs 100 for cataloguing, circulation, and OPAC; City is extending its system to cover acquisitions, but Heriot-Watt is not planning to use the financial control package offered. The circulation system is unusual in using a laser reader rather than the more common light-pen, and the

OPAC allows for searches by author, title, or classmark. Creating and editing full MARC records is difficult and is linked rather than integrated, while serials control will be provided by a link to the Pearl system developed by Blackwell's (formerly Perline). The Dynix system has been installed at Stirling and is replacing Aberdeen's in-house cataloguing and circulation systems. As yet the acquisitions and serials control modules have not been implemented in a university library. The Dynix OPAC is unusual in providing on-line reservations by readers, browsing of authority files rather than direct author or subject searches, and essentially command-driven searching.

Other systems have been installed on single sites. UMIST (University of Manchester Institute of Science and Technology) has adopted Adlib; Liverpool has implemented the cataloguing, OPAC, acquisitions, and circulation modules of IBM's Dobis-Libis system which is soon to be installed at Oxford as well. Bath uses the cataloguing, OPAC, circulation, and acquisitions modules of URICA, and is working toward the implementation of the serials module. The microcomputer-based system Librarian, marketed by Eurotec, is used at Buckingham for OPAC and cataloguing and some acquisitions information, with circulation to follow. Other small-scale integrated systems running on microcomputers, like Sydney's Micro Library, Pyramid's Calm, and Bookshelf, are not currently used in university libraries, though some of their modules are being considered for use as separate packages. Add to these BLCMP's BRS and SWALCAP's LIBERTAS and the extent of the choice facing university libraries is apparent.

A substantial number of libraries are likely to buy their first integrated system in the next few years to replace in-house systems or shared cataloguing and circulation. Some others are at or near the end of their Geac system's replacement cycle, usually considered to be about seven years. Choosing a new system is now a complex task, given the number of systems on the market and their different sizes, prices, and capabilities. Making such a choice is affected by the funding and decision-making structures of individual universities, and by the involvement of university staff from outside the library, which can vary considerably. But in most cases actually choosing system appears to be the responsibility of the library, within financial limits and legal or procedural guidelines laid down by the university.

The usual procedure is for the library to draw up specifications to be met by an automated system. These can change from a fairly brief and general account of the facilities and technical capabilities required to a full-scale and detailed account of the requirements, with considerable background information, as in the document drawn up by Oxford's Libraries Board. There is an increasing tendency for these specifications to be circulated and compared by libraries as part of the process of choosing a system. They usually distinguish between functions which must be available and those which would be desirable but not essential; on the whole, however, specifications tend to be treated as goals or ideals, rather than checklists directly related to the actual decision making. Other factors tend to play a more important role in reaching the final decision.

One of these factors is the effect of a library's existing system. If a commercial system is already installed, there is a strong incentive to continue with a new or upgraded version of it, rather than change to a different system altogether. The incompatibility of commercial systems is an important consideration here; even if the existing system can produce a transferable database in standard MARC format — which is not always the case — there are still all the associated files to be reconstituted on a new system. This is not so important a factor for libraries with in-house systems since incompatibility is inevitable for them, but it is important for libraries with aging Geac systems or with shared SWALCAP or BLCMP systems. It is hardly surprising that the latter group will probably all choose the standalone system offered by the supplier of their existing shared system, regardless of other factors.

The other major determining factor is, of course, the cost of the system. In a few cases, it has been possible for a library to choose its preferred system and then approach the university for an appropriate capital grant. More usually, though, the university sets a maximum amount which it is prepared to make available for library automation and libraries have to choose a cheaper system or try and raise further funds from other sources. Some have managed to get a reduced price, usually as a test site. External support has been hard to come by; only the most prestigious and well-known libraries can expect to raise money for automation from foundations and private donations. The UGC has not earmarked funds for library automation beyond the £1.5–2 million allocated in 1987 for improving network communications. Some Yorkshire libraries have considered the possibility of funding automation jointly, but found their requirements were not close enough for a joint approach to suppliers. Other avenues, such as raising money as part of an overall university appeal to benefactors, have been discussed but not yet tried.

Within the university, capital funds for library automation are often hard to come by in the present climate of financial stringency. Universities are not committed to the principle of a regular funding cycle for library automation, though this is now well-established for their computing services. As a result, the library's request for capital funds is usually treated as an exceptional circumstance, sometimes rejected entirely and sometimes agreed to in part, but rarely agreed to in full. Some universities lend the library the capital for automation, requiring it to be paid back over several years, with interest, from the recurrent grant. At least one library financed an integrated system in this way, while another bought a serials control package with a university loan against the income from photocopying. Another has been allowed to build up a balance in its recurrent account which can be used for meeting the capital costs of a new system. Several libraries are considering leasing systems rather than buying them outright, though the implementation of such arrangements would depend entirely on the financial policy of the individual university.

In general, the funding of automation in university libraries is unplanned, short-sighted, and far from adequate. Capital funding is left almost entirely to each university, or to the fund-raising skills of the library itself. The amounts required, especially if retrospective conversion is included as a capital cost, are well beyond the available equipment funds of most universities and are increasingly sought from other internal and even external sources. Even then, the capital provided is likely to be at the minimum level needed for a new system. There is also little provision for depreciating and writing off already purchased computer hardware and software over the course of its replacement cycle. Recurrent costs are also inadequately provided for, though they can involve substantial expenditure on software and hardware maintenance, and services from shared systems. Nevertheless, they come out of the library's recurrent budget, where they are in direct competition with books and periodicals for a share of a limited total amount.

SCONUL, in a 1986 submission to the UGC and the Computer Board for the Universities and Research Councils, recommended that one of these bodies take responsibility for funding library automation, on the grounds that the universities' normal equipment grants could no longer make adequate provision for it. An annual sum of £2.5 million was suggested by SCONUL, to cover a planned programme of amortisation and replacement over a cycle of about seven years.[3] This suggestion was not taken up by the bodies concerned, though the UGC did set aside funds for linking library computers to local area networks. The funding of library automation therefore remains precarious, with individual universities running into growing difficulties with providing capital funds and individual libraries having difficulty finding recurrent funds in their shrinking budgets. These funding problems come at a time when automation has become central to the efficient running of library services and vital to their quality and scope. Firm, better-planned funding of library automation is now one of the most important and urgent tasks facing university libraries in the immediate future. Otherwise, they will be stuck with second-rate or out-of-date systems just when information technology becomes dominant in many areas of university activity.

Funding constraints and an existing automated system are, then, the most important factors influencing the choice of a new system. Its facilities capabilities are usually less important. The type of hardware involved may become a major consideration if the university's computing service prefers, or wants to exploit its links with, a particular manufacturer of large computers. But this is essentially a question of cost rather than the relative merits of different machines. More important is the optimum size of the system; clearly, large libraries like Oxford and Edinburgh cannot use microcomputer-based system with a capacity of 100,000 records and would have serious difficulties with response time of all but the largest systems. But even where the capabilities of the system are theoretically adequate for a library's needs, poor performance may result from deficiencies in the design of the system or from insufficient processing power in a particular configuration. The system's specific facilities are less likely to exert a significant influence when a choice is made. Almost all of the commercial packages being marketed offer (or promise) the same range of modules, sometimes with one or two extras, and the choice among them is not likely to turn on such details as whether keyword searching is available or whether commitments in foreign currencies can be updated retrospectively. Some systems are undoubtedly more sophisticated and of higher quality than others, but these considerations are almost always secondary.

An interesting and important issue in this context is the extent to which a system is integrated, and the extent to which it will be implemented in an integrated way. Some of the available systems, like Geac, OCLC, and CLSI, are not fully integrated across all library functions; others, like URICA, are integrated but have not yet been fully implemented in a university library. The newest systems like LIBERTAS will be integrated but are still developing some of their modules. Many libraries have various in-house computer applications which are not integrated, and which have in some cases been maintained alongside commercial systems. Full-scale integration in university libraries is therefore still some way off, even for internal processes. External links are now moving quickly toward integration through the increasing use of connections to local area networks, and in the future these trends will converge to enable a single library terminal or workstation to be the means of access to the whole range of electronic applications.

As far as external links are concerned, a rapidly growing number of libraries make their own catalogues available on local area networks and hence on JANET, and consult the catalogues of other libraries by this means.⁴ Most have access to electronic mail and to on-line transmission of inter-library loan requests, and many have a facility for sending and receiving facsimile transmission. Most have access to other computers within the university, either through a local area network or by a direct terminal to a mainframe. All have access to commercial host systems for databases of various kinds. These external electronic applications are now spreading rapidly in university libraries, though at present their development is largely uncoordinated and unconnected.

The most common medium for making these applications available is the microcomputer, which can now be found in most libraries. There is a wide variety of different types of microcomputer: the IBM PC and its compatibles (especially Amstrad and Olivetti) are probably the most common, though incompatible makes such as BBC, Apple, and DEC Rainbow are often used. The range of uses for microcomputers is equally wide. Word processing and on-line searching are very frequently undertaken, as well as accounting and spreadsheet packages for financial and statistical analysis. Some microcomputers double as terminals to a larger library or university computer, others are used for retrospective conversion. There is an increasing use of microcomputers for inter-library loans, usually with on-line transmission of requests to the British Library's Document Supply Centre via ARTTEL, and for library databases of information about periodicals as part of cuts or re-evaluations of collections. Among the other applications are: book ordering, creation or editing of catalogue records, plans of library shelf arrangements, management of short loan collections, production of leaflets, and current awareness services. Aston even produces its annual report on an Apple Macintosh. Several libraries are considering buying commercial serials control packages which run on microcomputers; and Loughborough is already testing Faxon's Microlinx system.

Some of these applications are also available on most large automated systems, but many are not or are only in the process of being developed. Some use standard software but many are written or adapted in-house. A new layer of complexity is therefore being added to the already complicated picture in many libraries, where several unlinked automated systems are now being used for various activities. There are other technological developments already beginning to increase this complexity even further, notably electronic publishing, computer software as a part of library collections for loan, and the use of compact discs and other new media to store information, not to mention more specialized developments such as the computerized system developed at Newcastle for monitoring and analysing the numbers of users entering and leaving a library. This proliferation of computer applications will only become a source of confusion and wasted effort if it is allowed to continue unchecked at such a rapidly increasing rate.

It is clearly imperative for libraries to co-ordinate and control these developments, instead of letting them expand in an unplanned and ad hoc way. Linking and inter-connecting computer applications as part of a coherent automation policy is now an essential goal if they are to be put to the best possible use for the library and its users. From this point of view, the place of responsibility for automation within a library's decision-making structure is of great importance. Many libraries are only just beginning to face up to this issue. There has been a strong tendency to make provision for a specialist position to deal with the technical aspects of automated systems, often at a subordinate level within a technical services section, while leaving questions of planning and development to the chief librarian, deputy, or technical services librarian, and to the initiative of individual senior staff. This will not be adequate in the future; the way in which automation pervades all areas and its continually changing and developing nature make co-ordination and planning necessary on a library-wide scale. A growing number of libraries are endeavouring to meet this need by appointing a senior member of staff to have responsibility for the management of automation. Newcastle, for example, has a sub-librarian for automation, while Kent has a sub-librarian for automation and planning.

Automation, as it spreads into ever more applications, is increasingly difficult to contain within libraries' traditional organizational structures. It blurs the distinction between technical services and reader services, and between subject specialists and other staff. It tends to promote the integration of acquisitions and cataloguing sections, as database records are created when material is ordered. It increases the links between different sites or branches of a library, and often introduces problems of uniformity and standardization which were previously much less necessary. At the same time, greater decentralization of processes and functions is possible than with manual systems. These organizational changes as the result of increasing automation are often unexpected and unpredicted, and the pressures for change are likely to grow in the future as automation becomes even more pervasive.

Relationships between libraries are also affected by automation. Networks and shared systems draw libraries together in a greater awareness of common efforts toward standardization, and of each other's holdings and services. There is greater scope for co-operating and sharing information as communications links become more sophisticated. Libraries with the same commercial systems are encouraged to form user groups as a forum for voicing their views on the problems and future requirements of that system. Training, demonstrations, and assessments of systems are likely to bring together staff from different libraries. In these ways, automated systems have already proved themselves to be a means for bringing university libraries into closer contact with other university libraries and with libraries of other types, and this process will accelerate in the future.

At an intermediate level, automation can cause significant changes in the relationships between libraries within a federal or multi-level university system. At the University of London, plans to install the URICA system for all the university's more than 50 libraries which would be based at the central library in Senate House came to nothing when the University was unable to find capital and recurrent funding in 1986/87. In the aftermath, the largest college libraries are turning to separate LIBERTAS systems in a distributed network, a move with potentially major effects on the complicated structure of library provision within this federal university. At Oxford, the imminent installation of a single automated system under the direction of the Libraries Board seems certain to re-define the relationships between the Bodleian, the faculty and departmental libraries, and the college libraries. In all universities with several layers of library provision, which are usually unco-ordinated and value their independence, automation will sooner or later undermine the existing pattern of relationships between the different types of library.

Automation also has profound effects on the staff of university libraries. Most staff are not involved in choosing or planning for automated systems, at least at the decision-making level, though they often see a demonstration of short-listed systems and may be asked for their comments. Some libraries set up various working groups to co-ordinate the details of implementing a new system. Training staff to use it takes place in a variety of ways. Documentation is often poor and training by a system's suppliers is often an extra cost, so training tends to become something of a haphazard and gradual process in which much depends on the enthusiasm and ability of supervisory staff. The new procedures demanded by the automated system are often worked out by trial and error, rather than in a co-ordinated and well-organized way.

Effects on the duties of particular positions tend to be felt only gradually. Some jobs become more demanding: issue desk assistants have to learn a new set of routines, and subject librarians have to become familiar with on-line searching and other new ways of retrieving information. Acquisitions staff find themselves carrying out cataloguing tasks. Cataloguing is perhaps the most affected, as the use of external records enables most routine cataloguing to be performed by assistants rather than academic-related staff. The management of such changes requires a greater attention to the position and needs of individual staff members, as well as a more deliberate and planned approach to the definition of their duties. Automation tends to make job design a greater priority than it has been in libraries with long-established, largely manual procedures.

As far as staffing levels are concerned, it is a mistake to see automation as a way of reducing staff overall. Reductions are undoubtedly possible in some areas, such as cataloguing, but the general effect is to allow staffing patterns to be revised and staff transferred to other areas which are facing new or increasing demands. Most university libraries feel that automation has enabled them to cope with increased demands, especially for loans, at a time when staffing levels are being reduced because of government and university policy. This argument was successfully used at Nottingham, for example, where funds for automation were made available after the library insisted that only in this way could it continue to offer the same level of service after staff cuts. Libraries have resisted a generally held university view that automation will produce short-term reductions in staff. This resistance has not always been successful, however, and some libraries have found themselves with an automation allocation which is tied to a specific savings target for staff. That this situation has arisen less frequently than one might expect is the result of the universities' general financial position, which has made reductions in staff inevitable for most institutions, regardless of automation. In such a climate, the universities' main concern is reducing recurrent commitments, and automated library systems tend to be regarded, wrongly, as items of expenditure involving no commitments for the future. Staffing reductions, then, have not usually been directly linked to library automation.

Library users are generally less affected by automation. A few libraries have sought comments from their users as new systems are introduced, but many have relied on observing users rather than questioning them. OPACs appear to be generally popular; queues are common, and some libraries have had to install ropes to ensure that queues form in an orderly way. High tables for terminals, obliging the user to stand, are another way of encouraging shorter stays at an OPAC. Self-instruction and learning from one's peers seem to be very common, and a familiarity with computers is often assumed. Students especially seem to be the most enthusiastic users of automated library systems, while most criticism comes from academic staff, though not necessarily those who are older or belong to the arts faculty! Their complaints are sometimes founded on a view that the money spent on automation should be spent instead on books and periodicals, given the pressure on materials budgets. Other complaints regard poor response times from OPACs or apparently arbitrary changes to library rules and procedures caused by design constraints in the automated system.

Clearly, introducing automation requires a careful and well-planned approach to the very important area of public relations. But the library does not have to resort to publicizing automation as a novel and special feature, as has frequently happened with on-line searching, the other area of automation most noticeable to users. Too much publicity may lead to greater dissatisfaction if faults develop in the system, or may provoke a feeling that a particular service, or even the library itself, is irrelevant to an individual user's needs. Among university staff and students, there is a wide variety of attitudes toward automation and there are different levels of familiarity with it. The library needs to take account of these varying expectations among its users and must not assume that they will all be impressed with the new system.

The question of introducing a library's users to automation is becoming increasingly important with the growth of new applications for automated systems, and as organizational structures of libraries are changed by automation. The most fruitful approach would appear to involve stressing the nature and variety of the services the library can provide, rather than the way in which automation makes many of these possible. After all, automation is only a means to an end and publicizing specific aspects of automation puts the emphasis in the wrong place. It is the value and relevance of the services a library can provide which are important and should be publicized, not the way in which such services actually function. It is tempting, in a world which puts so much value on technological developments, to promote the library as a "high-technology" institution and to stress the extent to which it is automated. But such an approach is likely to discourage as many users as it attracts, except perhaps in the specifically technological universities. Automation should always be seen in the correct perspective, as no more than a means (albeit a powerful one) of enabling the university library to provide a range of services relevant to the needs of students and staff.

It is interesting to compare libraries with university computing services in this context. For many years, computing centres were primarily inward-looking institutions which did not promote their services in the university as a whole. They were a mystery to most departments other than those few which were frequent users of large computers. But more recently this has been changing under the impetus of the proliferation of microcomputers, a much higher level of computer use in the social sciences and arts, and the development of local area networks. Computing centres have become more aware of their role within the whole of the university, and have more actively advertised their services to potential users. There is an increasing emphasis on consultant services, the provision of applications packages and collections of data files, and support for users of microcomputers.

University libraries have had considerable contact with computing centres since the 1970s. The development of in-house systems has usually relied quite heavily on programming and technical expertise from the computing centre, and has often run on its machines. This has sometimes proved unsatisfactory, with software maintenance and development for the library being given a low priority, or a new make of mainframe creating problems when transferring library software. Some libraries have preferred to avoid such difficulties by using their own systems and programming staff and their own computer to run in-house applications. Another point of contact has been the growing tendency for libraries to provide space for terminals to the university mainframe, or microcomputers, for student use. Sometimes printers are provided as well. Libraries as different as Edinburgh, Southampton, and Salford have both terminals and microcomputers for student use. The main reason for this development is that the library is usually open longer than the computing centre; it also helps to make the centre's facilities available to a wider range of users.

At a more general level, there are now formal links established between university libraries and computing centres. SCONUL's Advisory Committee on Automation Policy has begun to hold an annual meeting with the Standing Committee of the Inter-University Committee on Computing (IUCC). The two bodies held a joint workshop at Durham in September 1986, aimed at discussing areas of mutual interest and suggesting further ways of collaboration. In the future there seems certain to be greater representation of each body on committees of the other; SCONUL is already represented on the Network Committee of the IUCC and on some of its Software Committee's working parties. A User Group for Libraries within the Joint Academic Network (JANET) was established in September 1986. This kind of formal co-operation at the national level is likely to increase rapidly in the immediate future.

In all these areas, contact between university libraries and computing centres has been growing steadily. But a development with major implications for the future of both institutions is now starting to take place, and is likely to result in their integration and joint management. At Westfield College, the librarian also took on the responsibilities of director of the computing centre; this was mainly a case of saving money after the previous director left, and there was little practical effect on the activities of the two bodies. At Salford, however, the librarian has also become director of computing services, with the eventual aim of integrating the two services and housing the computing centre's user support group in the library. The user support group is about to move into the main library building at Edinburgh, too, though with only a limited integration of its management.

That such moves are now possible is partly the result of a tendency in universities to regard the library and the computing centre as "academic services," an attitude also reflected in the combining of the Library Committee and the Computing Committee into a single Academic Services Committee. It is interesting to note that a few librarians, as at Sussex, are already responsible for the university's media services too, raising the possibility of a single post, Director of Academic Services. Libraries are regarded as having a strong interest in, and bias toward, automation similar to that found in computing centres. More fundamentally, though, there is a growing perception that a co-ordinated approach to information technology is necessary within the university if research is to be adequately supported. This has been expressed in a different way at Aston, where the director of library and information services was seconded to the post of pro-vice-chancellor for information technology.

The paths of libraries and computing centres are clearly converging, and there will undoubtedly be more mergers and co-ordinating appointments in the future, not just in the technological universities. But even among those librarians who are most enthusiastic about this trend there is unanimity that such mergers must be controlled by the library and that the library should not be subsumed into the computing services. University libraries, are, after all, more than the sum of their computerized systems. Certainly automation is now so pervasive in university libraries that it has become an integral part of most of their activities and processes. Many of their services depend on automation; their organization and procedures are increasingly determined and kept efficient by automation; much of their information for management, decision making, and financial control is provided by automated systems. And yet automation remains a means to an end. Computing centres exist because of automation, but libraries do not; their purpose is broader and their aims are more ambitious. They exist to provide the best possible means to achieve a high standard of research and teaching in universities, and to contribute to the intellectual development of their users in the broadest sense. Automation now has a vital part to play in achieving these aims, but it should not become an end in itself for university libraries.

REFERENCES

1. SCONUL. *Survey of funding cuts 1979/80-1984/85*; *Survey of funding 1984/85-1985/86*.

2. For automation in general, see: *State of the art of the application of new information technologies in libraries and their impact on library functions in the United Kingdom* (London: Library Technology Centre, polytechnic of Central London, 1987); and, Leeves, Juliet. *Library systems* (London: Elsevier, 1987). For specific systems and their applications in British university libraries, see the recent issues of *Vine* and *Program*.

3. SCONUL. *Annual report* 1986, pp. 59-74: "The needs of university libraries for computing systems and services."

4. *Directory of university library catalogues on JANET* (Brighton: University of Sussex Library for SCONUL, 1986).

Chapter 7

Relations with Other Libraries

The financial difficulties and changing circumstances of recent years have had their effect on university libraries' activities outside the university, as well as on their internal operations. There has been increasing pressure for co-operation, co-ordination, and rationalization across the whole range of university libraries. In part, this pressure has come from the university itself. The main motive has been to save money; the Vice-Chancellors of Bath and Bristol, for example, tried to insist on a rationalization of periodicals subscriptions for this reason, despite the objections of library staff and academics. But at a time when universities are being forced to co-operate in rationalization and co-ordination themselves, and are being urged to look outward to other universities and the community as a whole, there is a general climate of co-operation in the universities which is being passed on to their libraries.

National bodies are also promoting co-operation. The UGC made available a total of £1.5–2 million over the years 1987/88 and 1988/89, specifically for the purpose of improving computer networking in university libraries. The emphasis on linking libraries, rather than improving internal computer systems, was deliberate and reflected the UGC's interest in resource-sharing. In general, the UGC preferred not to deal directly with the issue of library co-operation directly, but the communications grant was a firm indication to the universities that co-operation between their libraries was a necessary consequence of overall policies toward the university system. The likelihood that the UGC would provide funds for CURL's joint index to the automated catalogues of the seven university research libraries was another clear indication of the value placed on co-operation.

A similar policy is being pursued by the government bodies concerned with libraries. The Library and Information Services Council (LISC), under the Office of Arts and Libraries, is encouraging libraries to co-operate more effectively on a local and regional basis, especially in the recommendations of its third report on the future development of libraries.[1] The main recommendation was for libraries to develop their own Library and Information Plans; these would be by county or region, based on the public library structure, but would cover all local libraries whether they were university, polytechnic, college, school, public, industrial, or society libraries. The libraries were to meet as a group and investigate the type of services they could offer each other. The Office of Arts and Libraries and the British Library began to fund pilot projects of this type in 1987.

Although these national activities gave a strong impetus to local co-operation, they did nothing to co-ordinate the funding of libraries, which remained split among several bodies: the UGC, the Office of Arts and Libraries, the local authorities, the Department of Education and Science, and the Welsh and Scottish Offices. In SCONUL's view, this lack of co-ordination means that the limited funds available are not always used in the best possible way; there needs to be a national co-ordinating body ensuring that collections of national value are maintained, unique material is preserved, and scholars have access to all relevant information.[2] LISC's (Library and Information Services Council) initiatives cannot meet these goals, nor is it or any other government body capable of making an overall assessment of the adequacy of libraries in Britain for research purposes. The UGC has made a point of not taking such a view, insisting that funding for university libraries is a matter for individual universities and should not be co-ordinated by the UGC. The university libraries are being given encouragement in co-operating and sharing their limited resources, but overall co-ordination and planning remains minimal.

In practice, however, this encouragement to co-operate has made comparatively little difference. University libraries already had various channels and organizations devoted to co-operation, and, while greater use has been made of these, there were only a few new initiatives. The only major new development was the emergence of

CURL. The third report of LISC, and the consequent work on local co-operative plans, is beginning to lead toward greater contact with public and other non-academic libraries, but this has not yet reached a significant level. Though greater co-operation by university libraries is taking place, the general framework has not been substantially changed.

The co-operation is still centred on SCONUL. With its small permanent secretariat and 16 advisory committees, SCONUL plays a very active role in co-ordinating and expressing the views of its members on a wide range of issues. Some of its committees are concerned with specialist material: American, Latin American, medical, Orientalist, Slavonic and East European, and manuscripts. Others deal with specific topics of library interest: automation, buildings, copyright, training and staffing, information services, inter-library loans, investigatory projects, national co-ordination, recurrent expenditure, and relations with the book trade. Many of these committees draw their membership from specialists outside the group of chief librarians, and many have a national role in their own right, not just through SCONUL as a whole. SCONUL is also represented on a wide variety of other national committees, mainly in librarianship and standards but increasingly in automation too. It is also being called on more frequently by the UGC, CVCP, government departments, LISC, and similar bodies to submit its views on specific issues at a national level.

Despite this enhanced national standing, SCONUL's internal affairs have become increasingly uncertain. This is especially evident with the withdrawals from membership of Bath and Glasgow at the end of 1982, followed by Stirling at the end of 1983, and with the formation of CURL during the same period as a separate forum for the seven largest university libraries, outside the scope of SCONUL. A thorough re-examination of SCONUL's activities was made by its Council at a special meeting at Hovingham in 1984, and detailed recommendations were drawn up for future work in 12 main areas: statistics, funding, training, acquisitions policies, conservation, centres of excellence, information technology, networking, copyright, scholarly communication, subject access, and charges. There were also recommendations dealing with the work and future of SCONUL's committees, and with its internal structure and external relationships.[3] The Hovingham meeting was clear evidence that SCONUL acknowledged its own problems and was making serious efforts to overcome them.

That there are still uncertainties in SCONUL today is a reflection of the many and complicated factors involved. The most obvious of these is the fee which SCONUL charges its members, calculated by adjusting a notional flat rate to allow for a library's relative size (usually in terms of student numbers). The notional rate was recently increased by 50%. With its fairly substantial charges, SCONUL is under pressure to demonstrate to libraries with shrinking budgets that it is giving them something tangible in return for their membership fee. The level of the fee is directly related to the cost of a permanent secretariat and its premises, which are also obliged to show their value.

SCONUL's structure also continues to cause difficulties. The large membership—69 in 1987—only meets twice a year for business sessions, usually concerned mainly with reports from the Council and the advisory committees. The Council itself has only ten elected members and meets formally five or six times a year. It has its own sub-committees: a House Committee dealing with detailed matters concerning the Secretariat, a Panel on Statistical Data, a Working Party on Preservation, and an occasional Panel on Membership and Structure. Policy, public statements, and activities are largely the responsibility of the Council and the full range of advisory committees, co-ordinated by the Secretariat. Matters requiring immediate or urgent action are usually dealt with informally by the chairman of the Council and the secretary, in consultation with other chairmen of committees or Council members as appropriate.

There is consequently a gap between the activities of the Council and those of the membership as a whole. Most of the business of the full meetings of all members is referred from Council or the advisory committees and is not concerned with formulating policy or making decisions. The Council, rather than the full membership, undertakes these functions. There is no requirement for consulting all members and obtaining their agreement before statements are issued and decisions taken by the Council, and individual members may find themselves in the position of disagreeing with one of

SCONUL's public statements but being criticized for supporting it by their university's vice-chancellor, who also disagrees with it. Members have the opportunity to play a more active role through the specialist advisory committees, but the members considered as a single body are very much on the fringe of SCONUL's decision making.

The Council itself is not appointed on a representative basis and tends to draw most of its members from the civic universities. In 1986, for example, none of the CURL libraries was represented on the Council, and neither were the technological universities. This is of considerable importance given the range of different types of library in membership of SCONUL. In addition to the various university libraries, ranging from large research libraries to small college libraries like St David's, Lampeter, there are the national libraries of Scotland and Wales and the British Library, and various government libraries like the Public Record Office, the Victoria and Albert Museum and the Science Museum. The Open University is a member, and so are many of the London colleges. There are also members from the Irish Republic as well as the United Kingdom. These different types of members have widely differing interests and priorities, and have differing expectations of SCONUL. The efforts of SCONUL to find a common ground on which to base its activities have left many libraries feeling dissatisfied. The large university research libraries felt that their interests were insufficiently catered to, and this was a major factor in the decision to set up CURL outside the framework of SCONUL. The technological libraries, in contrast, have been inclined to regard SCONUL as catering too much to the interests of larger libraries and not giving enough attention to their own preoccupations. The activities of SCONUL are therefore a continual balancing act between these varying expectations.

SCONUL has consistently resisted any movement toward splitting its membership into sub-groups based on type along the lines of CURL, and has held to the view that it exists to promote the common interests of all its members, rather than to make separate provision for each type of library. This, combined with the limitation of representation to chief librarians, makes it a unique forum for promoting the views of the university and national libraries as a group.

The problems produced by differing expectations within this group are the result not of the breadth of SCONUL's membership and its aims, but of the inadequacy of the administrative structure intended to put these aims into practice. This structure makes some libraries feel that they have little say in determining SCONUL's priorities and methods of operation; they are not drawn in to policy and decision making and have little chance of altering the way in which SCONUL works. Despite the Hovingham review, the machinery of SCONUL remains inadequate to meet the goals which SCONUL has set for itself.

The size of the membership and the existence of a permanent secretariat, have also pushed SCONUL in the direction of greater administrative formality. There has been a consequent proliferation of committees and paperwork. In 1986, a total of 292 reports, papers, and other documents were produced and circulated, while the agenda at business meetings runs to as many as 80 separate items. Many libraries find the sheer volume of business and documentation daunting and off-putting, and some are dissatisfied with what they see as an unnecessarily bureaucratic and cumbersome institution. But, given the present structure and the commitment to a single SCONUL voice on a wide range of issues, it is doubtful whether alternative methods of reporting and procedure would be workable. Less paperwork and less formality would seem to require a different organizational structure and probably a different scale of priorities for SCONUL's activities.

It is likely that such changes will result from the new generation of chief librarians which has emerged over the last few years. About 40% of the members of SCONUL at the end of 1987 had held their posts for less than six years—possibly the most rapid turnover of membership in the organization's history. It is still too early to see whether SCONUL will be changed fundamentally by the new attitudes and ideas which these new chief librarians are bringing to it. But there are already signs that they are expecting a body which concentrates on services to members more than it has in the past. The future development of SCONUL may well be in this direction, with a consequent reduction in its function of speaking nationally on behalf of its members and representing them on other bodies. Changes to the structure of SCONUL are likely to follow any alteration of its main areas of interest, though the precise effect on the relationship between the Council and the members and on the advisory committees cannot be predicted; the most that can be said for certain is that there will be a move away from administrative formality and proliferating paperwork. Under the direction of this new generation of chief librarians, SCONUL will certainly change considerably.

At present, although it places greatest emphasis on promoting nationally the interests of its members — through public statements, lobbying, and membership of committees — SCONUL does provide specific services. Among the most important of these are the meetings organized by or for SCONUL on specific topics of current interest; in some cases these are open to the wider library or academic community as well. In 1986, for example, there were seminars on such varied topics as on-line public access catalogues, conspectus, scholarly communication in the electronic age, and late medieval liturgical manuscripts. But the most important meetings were a joint workshop with the Inter-University Committee on Computing, and a seminar on the financial constraints affecting research collections in national and academic libraries. The proceedings of the latter were published.[4]

Among SCONUL's other publications, the most useful have been the surveys of the effects of funding cuts. These initially covered the period 1979/80 onward, but this series ended with 1984/85. A new survey of funding now covers the period 1984/85 to 1985/86.[5] These surveys measured the number of SCONUL libraries which had reduced their acquisitions, staffing, and services, and also investigated the extent to which additional money had been made available for new academic developments and automation. A table of total non-salary funds for each library over several years was also included. SCONUL's other major publication is the series of university library expenditure statistics, beginning in 1981/82, with the addition from 1984/85 of statistics on library operations.[6] Relying on forms completed by the libraries themselves and on sample surveys done by them, SCONUL is building up a database of statistical information about British university libraries from which comparative ratios can be derived. The usefulness of these ratios is limited by the various local factors which affect the figures, especially staff especially staff numbers and costs; at present, the comparative statistics are used in a highly selective and partial way by librarians and university administrators alike. Nor has SCONUL yet succeeded in having its statistics adopted as nationally authoritative by such bodies as the CVCP. The UGC's financial statistics remain the standard, even though from SCONUL's point of view they are compiled in an unsatisfactory way. There are also limitations to the coverage of SCONUL's statistics; several of the largest libraries do not participate in the survey of library operations, and several insist that their financial statistics be kept confidential.

In general, while SCONUL's firm commitment to building up a range of statistical information has had the backing of a majority of its members, there has also been a strong element of scepticism about the usefulness of this work and about the uses which may be made of it. It is interesting in this context to note that before the foundation of SCONUL in 1950, the then librarian of Cambridge, H. R. Creswick, wrote that he hoped the new body "will not ask its members to embark upon the compilation of returns, statistical or otherwise, or replies to elaborate questionnaires. . . . the days are only too full already."[7] The compilation of statistics, despite the amount of time this requires, is these days a political necessity, given that most decision making by governments and universities makes frequent, though highly selective, use of statistics. In this sense, SCONUL's efforts to compile fuller and more accurate figures relating to university libraries are well worthwhile, since they provide libraries with their own statistical ammunition. But the possibilities for selectivity and misinterpretation of statistics have been increased, and will increase further as performance indicators are developed. Some libraries are unhappy with SCONUL's current involvement in trying to develop performance indicators from its financial and operational statistics.

Another important service provided by SCONUL has been its trainee scheme. Prospective postgraduate students of librarianship can apply to SCONUL for a year's post as a trainee in a university library, to help meet the entry requirements for their course. In 1986, there were 617 applications for a total of 70 available posts; in 1985, applications had been as high as 862. Applicants are asked to state which libraries they would prefer, and the libraries themselves make their own choices; the SCONUL secretariat plays a coordinating role. Only 26 of the SCONUL libraries participated in the trainee scheme in 1986. Some of the others prefer to recruit trainee library assistants directly, sometimes on the grounds that applications were unlikely to include this library as one of the preferred choices, or because trainees of better quality could be recruited locally. Some libraries did not want to be bound by the need to rotate SCONUL trainees through different sections of the library to give them a range of experience. Quite a few have been forced to abolish trainee posts altogether as an immediate and easy response to demands from the universities for staffing cuts. SCONUL commissioned a survey of the trainee scheme in 1987 to assess the opinions of students, library schools, and employers. Among the options being considered for the future is an extension of the scheme to polytechnic libraries. The trainee scheme has undoubtedly made a very valuable contribution to professional education in the past, but the stagnation of professional posts in university libraries and the financial difficulties of most of them have now combined to make this contribution a general one, rather than a way of training future academic-related staff for university libraries.

SCONUL also provides its members with an important informal service—the opportunity to meet other chief librarians and to share and discuss current problems and issues with them. In 1987 the format of the main SCONUL meeting was changed to allow for this type of practical discussion based on short papers, and SCONUL can be expected to devote more attention to this in the future. The new generation of chief librarians is likely to encourage such moves; there has already been an "exchange of experiences" seminar for new chief librarians, and also a proposal to establish a training programme for senior library management along the lines of a staff college. Detailed profiles of individual university libraries have been compiled, and one of their uses is intended to be as a source of information for other libraries. Another move in the direction of services for SCONUL members has been an electronic-mail network within SCONUL, improving communications at a reduced cost to individual libraries. Practical and information services like these to members are likely to become an important part of SCONUL's activities in the future.

For all the tensions and uncertainties currently evident, SCONUL remains an institution of great value. This is evident above all in the way in which it stresses the common interests of all university libraries, however much these libraries differ in practice. As a link between them and the national libraries it is probably less successful and only integrates their common interests in special meetings or advisory committees, instead of in its whole organization and range of activities. But offers a unique forum for co-ordinating the needs and interests of a wide range of libraries concerned with providing services and collections for researchers. At present, this is done in a variety of ways: public statements, lobbying, seminars, statistics, and services aimed at improving the skills and knowledge of chief librarians. In the future there is likely to be more emphasis on the last of these, probably linked with less administrative formality and a revised organizational structure.

If SCONUL is uncertain about its future direction, CURL (the Consortium of University Research Libraries) is rather more certain. It brings together a much smaller and more homogeneous group of libraries, those in universities with over 10,000 students, covering Cambridge, Edinburgh, Glasgow, Leeds, London, Manchester, and Oxford. It has no permanent administration and a minimum of paperwork, and is concentrating on practical initiatives of relevance to its members. It is careful to make public statements only when there is unanimity among members, and to consult the universities' vice-chancellors before making such statements. It holds quarterly meetings, and also has a Technical Officers Group which is concerned primarily with issues of automation.

Among CURL's current projects are a comparison of staffing patterns and grades, and a survey of the major microform collections of its members. But by far its most important work has been setting up a central joint index to the machine-readable catalogue files of its members, with funding from the Wolfson Foundation and the UGC. The files and the joint index are held on a computer at Manchester, and will be accessed through JANET using local microcomputers and the software written for Cambridge's OPAC. The initial size of these files will be nearly 1 1/2 million records, and new records will be added by magnetic tape at first, with file transfer through JANET a future possibility. The initial aims are to provide the CURL libraries with information about each other's holdings and to provide a source of MARC records for them. But the eventual good is to make these records freely available to all university libraries. After the failure of past attempts to create a national database (the UK Library Database System), the CURL project is of great importance for future co-operation between university libraries.

Other co-operative bodies which involve university libraries are organized on a regional basis. Some are exclusively for such libraries, as is the case with MOYUL and S$_3$RBK. MOYUL (the Meeting of Yorkshire University Libraries) now also includes Durham and Newcastle, while S$_3$RBK covers those universities in the southeast outside London: Southampton, Surrey, Sussex, Reading, Brunel, and Kent. These organizations provide an opportunity for chief librarians within a region to exchange information and discuss current issues and problems. Their subordinate staff may meet too in areas such as acquisitions or reference work. The most common subjects for discussion tend to be reciprocal borrowing and reading rights, staff training, periodicals subscriptions, and automation.

Other co-operative bodies involve all the major libraries in a local area along the lines recommended by the third LISC report. One of the best known of these is the Birmingham body BCOP (Birmingham Libraries in Co-operation), which has organized staff exchanges, visits, joint seminars, and a union catalogue, but has had little success with issues like joint storage and rationalizing periodicals subscriptions. A different approach is taken by Hampshire's HATRICS, which has about 400 members including many companies and government bodies, and concentrates on training, inter-library loans, and information about subjects like patents and standards. These organizations tend to be fairly informal, and to rely on subscriptions for their funds. At an even more informal level is local co-operation with other academic libraries, chiefly polytechnics. Those university libraries with a nearby polytechnic usually have some co-operative activity with it in reciprocal rights and possibly training. Manchester, for example, has meetings of the five academic libraries in the city, while a research project sponsored by the British Library is looking at increasing co-operation between five academic libraries in Leicestershire and Nottinghamshire.

Other libraries, like Hull, are looking at greater co-operation with a local college. These different types of grouping tend to overlap; Sussex, for example, as well as being a member of S₃RBK, takes part in co-operative bodies known as SASLIC (Surrey and Sussex Libraries in Co-operation) and the Society of Sussex Librarians, which has a Standing Committee on Co-operation.

Co-operation in England varies considerably between regions. In Scotland and Wales, however, there is scope for greater uniformity and national co-operation. Scotland's Working Group on Library Co-operation covers the eight universities, the public libraries of Edinburgh and Glasgow, and the National Library of Scotland, which provides the secretariat. Its current work is centered on applying the Conspectus method of collection assessment to these libraries, with the aim of making the results available on-line. It is also working toward a Scottish network of on-line catalogues, possibly with the Conspectus results as a subject guide. The Welsh college libraries are already linked formally as constituent members of the University of Wales and are now considering a national co-operation plan for Wales involving other libraries, especially the National Library of Wales. There is also the possibility of co-operative automation between some of the colleges.

If co-operation on the regional or national level is often difficult to achieve, is no less so within single, very large universities. The complexities of co-operating in a large federal institution are well illustrated by London University, with its more than 50 libraries. There is now a growing move away from a centralized structure for this federal system; previously automated cataloguing and circulation had been the responsibility of the Central Library Services, which also provided co-ordination in training and a union catalogue of periodicals. Now the larger college libraries are making their own decisions about automation and are also pushing for changes to the composition and responsibilities of the Library Resources Coordinating Committee, which is the university body appointed to oversee the whole range of libraries. Co-operation in collection development has been the task of this Committee's subject sub-committees, but they vary greatly in effectiveness. One major success has been the rationalization of responsibility for maintaining research collections in the sciences, now centred on University College. The place of the central University Library within this changing picture is uncertain, especially in view of the UGC's determination to reduce sharply the funds available for central services in the University of London. A review of the Library in 1987 recommended that it become the University Humanities Library.

A similarly complicated and difficult situation has recently been reviewed at Oxford, where library provision is divided between the Bodleian and its dependencies and the faculty, departmental, and college libraries. There has been considerable co-operation between most of these in such areas as collection development and union lists. The planned automation will take place across the first three groups of library, with several of the colleges showing an interest as well. But the formal machinery for co-ordinating this richness of libraries is far from adequate. The Libraries Board is responsible for dividing the available funds between the Bodleian and the faculty libraries, and for the co-operative automation programme, but its relationship with the Curators of the Bodleian has been uneasy and ill-defined. Major changes to the arrangements for co-ordinating library provision will be needed before closer and more effective links between the different types of library in Oxford will be possible.

In addition to all these relationships between university libraries and other libraries, there is another very important relationship — with the British Library. The British Library has had to operate within the constraints of reduced funding in real terms; it has placed much more emphasis on marketing its services and raising revenue from them. Other major changes have been an overhaul of its organizational structure, a more integrated approach to the development and management of its collections, and the beginning of construction of its new building on the St Pancras site. All these lines of development were endorsed in the Library's strategic plan for the period 1985 to 1990.[8]

The British Library continues to be of great importance to university libraries in several ways. Many use its bibliographic services, and UKMARC records are at the heart of many library databases; in some cases, this use is indirect, through BLCMP or SWALCAP, but in others it is directly from BLAISE. The new link between the British library and the Joint Academic Network may increase this direct use at a time when the Library's catalogue production service LOCAS is being phased out and its university library users are having to reconsider their arrangements for automated cataloguing. The British Library's adoption of Conspectus as its method of collection assessment is also of growing relevance to university libraries; those in Scotland are already making use of Conspectus themselves and others are considering doing so. In addition, the collecting policies of the British Library are now documented and available to university libraries as part of their information for making decisions about their own collections.[9]

The Library's support for research projects attached to university libraries continues to be a valuable way of developing special services or resources; its grants for special projects in listing, cataloguing and preservation have also assisted several university libraries. But their greatest use of the British Library is for the lending services of the Document Supply Centre, which is their automatic first choice for almost all their inter-library loan requests. Several university libraries have, however, voiced their concern that because of its shortage of funds the British Library is making growing use of a single copy for both reference and lending, instead of providing a copy for each purpose. With all these links between the British Library and the university libraries, there are various formal channels for exchanging views, of which SCONUL is the most important, even though the national libraries are less than adequately integrated into its activities and organization.

University libraries in Britain have links with a wide variety of other libraries, ranging from the British Library to small local libraries, though the extent and effectiveness of co-operation vary greatly. Union lists of periodicals are a frequent co-operative activity, sometimes produced within a single complicated university library system, as at Cambridge, London, and Oxford, and sometimes on a regional basis. A good example of the latter is the Serials Union List for South Yorkshire, which covers Sheffield's university, polytechnic, city, and industrial libraries; it is maintained by the university library, which is developing it from a microfiche list into an on-line database. Up-to-date holdings details are essential in such lists, together with information on library locations and lending policies. Arrangements for maintaining union lists and catalogues, and making them available, tend to be informal and improvised.

Co-operative approaches to staff training and development are quite common. Regular visits to other nearby libraries, but not necessarily academic ones, are one way of doing this. Exchanges are less frequent, though trainee library assistants may be seconded for a short period to another library, as at Reading. Southampton is planning for possible exchanges of junior staff with a local college of liberal arts and institute of higher education. Joint training schemes are not unusual; Warwick University and Coventry Polytechnic have such an arrangement, while London has a centrally organized programme for its many libraries. BCOP organizes all these types of co-operation in training, as well as joint seminars on current issues, through its Staff Training Working Party. These co-operative efforts in staff training and development are especially valuable at a time of professional stagnation in university libraries, at both the academic-related and senior library assistant levels.

Another important area of co-operation is reciprocal rights for readers. These are far from automatic between university libraries; even within London University a general policy on reciprocal use is only now being worked out, and some college libraries have had to negotiate their own bilateral agreements. This type of co-operation exists between many university libraries within a particular geographical area, such as the members of MOYUL. Reciprocal arrangements between university and polytechnic libraries in the same city are common. But other types of library are not included, though a few university libraries are considering extending such arrangements to local colleges. Borrowing rights are almost always limited to academic staff and postgraduate research students; other students may have reading rights only, and sometimes must make an individual case to obtain these, as in the arrangement between Edinburgh and Heriot-Watt. The increasing numbers of postgraduate course students are a growing problem which has yet to be resolved — under existing agreements they are usually entitled to reading rights only. Students also have reading rights during the university vacation at their local university library. In general, though, there is considerable scope for increasing and extending co-operation between academic libraries over the question of reciprocal rights for library users.

Co-operation in collection development and management has, on the whole, met with little success, despite the strong support of some university administrators who see this as a way of saving money. It has been most successful within a large federal university like London, or where there are several different types of library provision, as at Cambridge and Oxford. Collecting responsibilities at a research level are shared and co-ordinated within London University, to a greater or lesser extent, by the subject sub-committees of the Library Resources Co-ordinating Committee. The more specialized libraries, like the British Library of Political and Economic Science and the School of Slavonic and East European Studies, co-operate to avoid overlap of their collections. At Cambridge and Oxford, holdings of scientific periodicals are co-ordinated in such a way that a unique title held in any of the departmental libraries cannot be cancelled without notifying a central committee.

There is very little successful co-operation of this type between university libraries or with other types of library. Exeter has been looking at rationalization and sharing some periodicals subscriptions with the Plymouth Polytechnic, but Bath and Bristol found such measures would be too difficult for them to implement. Some libraries (such as those in S_3RBK) consult with others before making periodicals cancellations, but there is usually insufficient time to make co-operative arrangements. Some, as in Scotland, consult before purchasing expensive items; the Scottish libraries have tried to define areas of interest, especially for older material. Acquisitions librarians within some groups of university libraries, such as MOYUL, hold their own meetings. The adoption of Conspectus by the British Library and the 11 major Scottish libraries is an important new aspect of co-operation in collection development, since it offers a standard technique, whatever its shortcomings, as a basis for documenting and comparing current collecting policies and existing collections. The eventual goal suggested by SCONUL is a nationally co-ordinated pattern of collection development, with much greater selectivity in most university libraries, and with the largest libraries acting as more comprehensive centres of excellence; such co-ordination presupposes a standard method like Conspectus. Whether such co-ordination is possible at a time of severe financial constraints remains to be seen.

Co-operation in inter-library lending continues to be founded firmly on the British Library's Document Supply Centre, which is almost invariably the first source for loan requests of university libraries. Loans by these libraries, other than those which act as backup libraries for requests unsatisfied by the British Library, are comparatively small in volume, but very few libraries have had to reduce them because of cuts in funding. The university libraries are usually also members of their regional inter-lending networks, but make much less use of them, mainly for books. Co-operative transport schemes are common within these regions for distributing material, including material from the Document Supply Centre. One of the region, the Northern Regional Library System, is even involved in acquiring and promoting a computerized system for measuring library admissions.

Three of the regions are also involved in the Viscount Project for developing an on-line inter-library loans network. This project is centred in the London and South East Library Region (LASER), and aims to provide on-line access to a database containing bibliographic records and holdings for the monographs held by members of LASER, the North Western and South Western Regional Library Systems, the lending services of the National Library of Scotland, and the British Library's Document Supply Centre. As well as providing bibliographic and holdings information, the Viscount network will also allow electronic transmission of messages within regions, between regions, and eventually to the Document Supply Centre. Once the Viscount network is fully operational, it will undoubtedly have an important effect on national inter-lending patterns, though it is too early to say whether university libraries will prefer it to the Document Supply Centre as their first choice for requesting loans of monographs.

The Viscount Project is also an example of the vital role being played by automation in increasing co-operation. This continues to apply especially to shared cataloguing; despite the contraction of SCOLCAP to the level of an essentially internal system of the National Library of Scotland, BLCMP and SWALCAP remain successful examples of this kind of co-operation. SWALCAP has changed character considerably and has been, since January 1986, a private limited company with the name SWALCAP Library Services Ltd. This change from a consortium was intended to provide a more streamlined and flexible management capable of developing and marketing a stand-alone system as well as maintaining the original shared cataloguing and circulation services. The new company can also offer its employees commercial salaries and contracts rather than university ones, and is no longer located within Bristol University. It can sell its new LIBERTAS stand-alone system to outside customers without having to involve them in its membership; the original members are now shareholders and are not obliged to add new members with an equal voice and a veto, which had been part of the idea of a consortium. The co-operative services are still being provided to existing users, but the emphasis now is less on co-operation and more on finding new customers for the stand-alone system and possibly for the supply of bibliographic records.

BLCMP, on the other hand, is a co-operative, with a membership nearly double that of SWALCAP's shareholders. New users of BLCMP products become members of the co-operative and have a say in the way it is run. BLCMP too has developed a stand-alone integrated system and is placing less emphasis on its shared services, but it is doing this within a framework different from SWALCAP's commercial one. The arrangements for decision making appear to be somewhat confused and unclear in BLCMP; priorities for systems development are a source of tension and conflict between the User Groups, concerned with improving existing operational details, and the Council (which consists of the chief librarians of each member library) and the elected Board of Directors, who apparently would prefer the development of management information systems as a higher priority. There are difficulties resolving these differences into a single development plan for BLCMP's systems staff. As a co-operative BLCMP can be more responsive to the needs of all its users, but at the cost of having a much greater variety of opinions to try and harmonize.

BLCMP and SWALCAP are part of the national Co-operative Automation Group, which also includes representatives of LASER, SCOLCAP, and BLAISE. Although the group's work toward a national database came to nothing, it is still active in arranging licensing schemes for the exchange of bibliographic records between its members and in promoting common standards for exchanging and retrieving records. Its other interests include the technical aspects of database structures and communications between databases, and the legal and commercial issues involved in sharing data and making records available.

Co-operation through automation at a national level is also taking place through the Joint Academic Network (JANET), linking the local area networks of the universities. In late 1986, 16 university libraries had made their on-line catalogues available through JANET, and the number is certain to rise rapidly in the near future with earmarked UGC funding.[10] York already offers its users access to some of these other catalogues as part of the standard OPAC menu. As well as providing information about holdings, the catalogues on JANET are being used for transferring records between libraries, notably from Cambridge to Oxford as part of the latter's pilot automation project. The CURL database and joint index will rely on JANET to provide access for member libraries, and eventually to transfer local files to the central database.

JANET provides a link to and from other libraries outside the university system through gateways joining it to the public PSS network. In 1987 the British Library was linked to JANET, making it possible for university libraries to send inter-loan requests directly through JANET to the Document Supply Centre, and allowing a direct link to BLAISE. JANET is also an avenue for electronic mail, and many university libraries now have mailboxes on the network. They also have access to the public electronic mail system Telecom Gold, through SCONUL's overall subscription. Use of electronic mail is still in its infancy in British university libraries and so is use of facsimile transmission, but their use will undoubtedly rise quickly in the next few years.

In these ways, automation is proving to be one of the most effective means of encouraging co-operation and closer contact between the university library and other libraries. New applications are sure to emerge in the future, such as the proposed on-line Conspectus for Scotland. Automation enables co-operation to take place over greater distances, especially in fulfilling the university library's aim of making available materials needed for research, and providing information about their location. Local co-operation, in contrast, has tended to be limited to activities which are invisible to the user, such as staff training, or to attempts to reduce the effects of cuts by sharing them, as with periodicals cancellations. Its greatest relevance to users has been in reciprocal rights for using other local libraries; the value of this depends entirely on the existing geography of library provision—Exeter and East Anglia, for example, have much less scope for co-operation in their local areas than Aston or Salford do in theirs.

Co-operative action must enable libraries to offer their users extra services which would otherwise be impossible, rather than simply try to share the difficulties of maintaining services. The attitudes of users are an important part of this process; too many academics still tend to expect self-sufficiency in their university library, either because they used a large research library for their research or because librarians are often still aiming at such a goal themselves, regardless of present realities. The highest priority in co-operation by university libraries must be providing access to research materials wherever they are held, since most libraries can no longer hope to maintain adequate research collections themselves. The regional co-operative plans suggested by LISC have little to offer in this context, except in the few largest cities with public and university research libraries. A national initiative like JANET is far more important, and most university libraries should aim to build its use into their normal pattern of services, educating their users to regard the library as part of a national network, rather than an increasingly unsuccessful attempt at self-sufficiency.

REFERENCES

1. Library and Information Services Council. *The future development of libraries: Progress through partnership and planning* (London: H.M.S.O., 1986).

2. SCONUL. Advisory Committee on National Co-ordination. *Minutes*, 86/12 (SCONUL document 87/23).

3. SCONUL. *Annual report* 1984, pp. 57-61 (summary recommendations); *Issues facing academic libraries* (London: SCONUL, 1985) (summaries of papers).

4. *Research collections under constraint and the future co-ordination of academic and national library provision* (London: SCONUL, 1986) (British Library R&D report 5907).

5. SCONUL. *Survey of funding cuts 1979/80–1984/85*; *Survey of funding 1984/85–1985/86*.

6. SCONUL. *University library expenditure statistics*, 1981/82– ; *SCONUL statistical database part II: Library operations*, 1984/85–

7. Bowyer, T.H. "The founding of the Standing Conference of National and University Libraries (SCONUL)", in: *University library history*, ed. James Thompson (London: Bingley, 1980), p. 218.

8. British Library. *Advancing with knowledge: The British Library strategic plan 1985-1990* (London: British Library, 1985).

9. British Library. *Conspectus in the British Library* (London: British Library, 1986).

10. *Directory of university library catalogues on JANET* (Brighton: University of Sussex Library for SCONUL, 1986).

Conclusion

For British university libraries, recent years have been a period of sharp and often painful contraction. Cuts in government funding for the universities began with the 1981/82 academic year and have continued since then in a generally unpredictable way. Since 1986/87 funding has been much more selective, with some institutions having their grants cut in cash terms and others having theirs increased in real terms. For the universities, whose recurrent expenditure is mostly on staffing, the main effect has been losses of many academic posts, usually through early retirement. As a consequence, courses have been dropped, departments closed or merged, and subject coverage reduced. The general mood has been one of confusion and demoralization in the face of this sudden and unpredictable change for the worse.

University libraries have not escaped the effects of these cuts. Indeed, they appear to have been badly affected, with their share of university recurrent expenditure falling considerably. They too have found reductions in staff numbers a continual necessity. Posts at all levels have been abolished or frozen, and substantial reorganization of staffing structures has often been needed to try and cover for these losses. Many libraries have had to reduce their operating hours or to open without services because of insufficient staff. Enquiry desks and service points have frequently been left unstaffed during standard office hours. For a considerable number of libraries, staff numbers are inadequate to allow for covering of absences through illness. Staff losses have been heavy at the clerical and non-academic level, because the higher turnover there has enabled quick savings to be made. At the academic-related level, substantial reductions — mainly through early retirement — have been combined with a general stagnation in which there is little movement of staff to other libraries and virtually no recruitment of new academic-related staff. A growing class of senior library assistants, who are qualified to hold academic-related posts but have virtually no prospect of doing so, has added to the serious problems in staffing.

Because university libraries, unlike academic departments, are mainly hierarchical organizations with service and functional responsibilities, the staff cuts have had a more serious effect on their overall condition. Reduced funding has also greatly affected their budgets for acquiring library materials. The cuts coincided with a period when the value of the pound against foreign currencies fell sharply, making purchases from overseas much more expensive. The inflation rate for books and periodicals continued to rise steeply, well above even the largest cash increases in library expenditure. As a result, book purchases have declined considerably in many libraries, there have been frequent large cancellations of periodicals subscriptions, and the ratio of the budget between books and periodicals has risen sharply in favour of the latter. In general, libraries have been able to afford a much lower proportion of the new academic books and periodicals published.

These substantial reductions in acquisitions and staff have been accompanied by an increase in charges for, and limits to, services like inter-library loans and on-line searching. These trends seem bound to continue in the immediate future, at least for those libraries whose universities are doing poorly in the new formula-based selective funding. In the universities which are benefitting most under these arrangements, libraries will still be under pressure to contain staffing costs and reduce numbers, while acquisitions budgets may be more generous than before. In general, the erosion of services and collections in university libraries will continue, though perhaps less rapidly and in a less unplanned way.

These cuts in funding have undoubtedly had a serious and dramatic effect on the quality of services and collections in British university libraries. But at a deeper level there are trends at work which will also have a great effect on the very nature of the university library, rather than on its quality alone. Universities themselves are changing markedly in character, partly as a result of government policy and partly because of the universities' own initiatives, individually and through the CVCP and UGC. The cuts in funding were no more than a lever used to start this process of change. The funding of universities has become tied to government insistence on greater accountability. Performance indicators and staff appraisal are being introduced to measure the performance of universities, and research results now determine how a substantial proportion of government funds are allocated. This selectivity will be extended further with the increasing rationalization of subject coverage—in research and teaching—between universities. The result may well be that some universities undertake no research at all, and teach only specific subjects determined on a national basis. Behind this lies the government's basic view, which regards universities primarily as institutions for the output of qualified manpower and research results in specific fields, according to the country's economic needs. The new system of funding by contracts between each university and the proposed Universities Funding Council is intended to establish this view as the basis of all financial decisions about universities.

Within this national framework, the universities are having to reorganize themselves considerably, in order to maintain their share of the total funding available. The ways in which they run their affairs, organize themselves, and allocate funds to their constituent parts are being changed and streamlined to reduce the amount of administrative machinery and to ensure that general decisions are made quickly. A context for decision making has been provided by formal, detailed plans for the future, which have been required by the UGC as a condition of further funding. Individual departments are being given more authority and flexibility in deciding the precise division of their share of the budget within the general planning framework. The result is an institution which bears a greater resemblance to a commercial company than to the universities of the past.

The position of the library within the university as a whole is changing profoundly. Libraries are having to find a new place in the structure of decision making, often without formal contact with the central group which makes budgetary decisions. The Library Committee faces a merger into a broader committee covering academic services. The library itself is being given greater flexibility in making use of its total budget, with a consequent need to set priorities between staffing and expenditure on materials and services. Acquisitions are tending to be determined almost entirely by academics, under a formula giving faculties or departments a single sum for books and periodicals. For most libraries, new materials are largely limited to those required for specific current courses and research, within the university's plan. The library is increasingly seen as provider of academic services, and is required to tailor its activities closely to current university plans and policies, rather than to follow independent, and possibly wider, guidelines of its own. When most universities no longer aim to provide a general education across a broad range of subjects, and emphasize instead specific subjects linked to specific careers, the library is under strong pressure to follow the same path. There is no place for the university library considered as a general instrument of education, parallel to, but in an important way separate from, the academic departments.

As one of the academic services, the library is increasingly involved in plans for their gradual convergence. Librarians are assuming responsibility for computing services and media services within the university, raising the possibility of a future integrated academic service covering all these areas. The rapid increase in automation in university libraries is one of the factors contributing to this development. If basic services like circulation have not broken down entirely under the pressure of staff cuts, this has been largely due to automated systems which have coped with rising demand from users in the same period. Automation is also showing increasingly successful results when applied to co-operation between libraries, both by extending it to new fields and by improving it in the few areas where it had previously been a substantial success.

Another effect of automation has been to make collection management gradually less difficult. Using automated systems, libraries are finding it easier to link acquisitions with circulation, and in this way to tailor collecting policies to actual use of material in individual subject areas; this fits in closely with the idea of providing almost exclusively for current needs. This kind of use analysis can also be the basis for systematically withdrawing and relegating the least-used stock, along the lines proposed in the Atkinson report in 1976. Such continuous relegation has not yet been put into practice, not so much because of objections to the principles on which the report was based, but as a result of a spate of extensions and new library buildings under the new norms for size laid down by the same report. There has been some rationalization of small areas of collections between libraries as part of comparatively minor rationalization of subjects at the university level, but this is likely to become more frequent and substantial in the future. Automation will also help to make this process of withdrawing and transferring collections less cumbersome and difficult.

Automation is one area where university libraries have had some success in obtaining direct earmarked funding from the UGC, bypassing the universities. There has also been an extra, non-recurrent grant for library materials, though some universities have not treated this as additional to the recurrent allocation they make to their libraries. But, in general, provision for university libraries is not nationally co-ordinated, though the pressures for this to happen are increasing. Funding library automation on a regular cycle is beyond the budgets of many universities and may eventually have to be a national responsibility, in the same way that the Computer Board provides for university computing services. National co-ordination of libraries' collecting responsibilities may be the best way to overcome the inadequacies of individual acquisitions budgets. As yet, however, there is no sign that this is likely to happen, especially since extra funding would almost inevitably be necessary.

At the moment, then, the future of university libraries depends on the attitude of each university's decision makers, administrators, and (to a lesser extent) academic staff generally. In a substantial number of universities, it is clear that the library is regarded as unnecessarily expensive and of doubtful value, and there is little sympathy or special provision for the library when budget allocations and staffing targets are made. Though libraries have more freedom dividing up their budget, they are having to do this within a much more constricted general framework, which will soon be expressed in terms of meeting and maximizing government contracts for teaching and research in specific fields. Far from being the intellectual heart of the university—the stock phrase used in the past with varying degrees of appropriateness—the library faces the prospect of becoming an ancillary service with a restricted budget, responsible for little more than providing adequate access to materials needed for current research and teaching.

This is the real challenge facing British university libraries. The "holdings versus access" debate is secondary in comparison, since most libraries have already been forced to turn away in practice (if not consciously) from the idea of local collections which are as self-sufficient as possible, and catalogued and bound to a high standard. At the same time, however, many are limiting access through inter-library loan or on-line retrieval, and university policy on staff reductions is limiting the development of services. The more fundamental need is to convince academics and administrators alike that the library is vital to the continued health of the university. Government funding, research contracts, and overseas students are all directly related to good results in teaching and research; without a library of high quality, such results are impossible. The precise mixture of services, collections, and access needed to produce this quality will vary with the character of each university, and between different sections of the university. But the library's immediate goal is the same: to show that it is an essential part of the research and teaching methods of the university.

In the present context, this will require a coherent and realistic plan for the future, linked to the university's own plan. The aim should be for the library to have as much control as possible over setting its own priorities, especially in areas like staffing and collection development. A more flexible organizational structure will also be a necessity if the conflicting demands of staff cuts, greater accountability, and development of services are to be met. Budgets will also need to be restructured as priorities change and as the scope and complexity increase with one-line, cost-centred budgeting. A greater range of statistical information will also be necessary—partly for management decision making and partly in view of the likelihood that performance measures will be derived from such data.

This is the context within which university libraries will have to make decisions if they aim to be more than a secondary service with a narrowly defined role within the university. Just as the government is calling on the universities to re-examine their basic aims and nature, so the universities are gradually forcing their libraries to do the same. Unless the library can clearly articulate a coherent vision of its own future, the narrowly functional view emerging in the university will prevail by default. A decline into mediocrity and into a purely ancillary status will become the fate of the library. The events of the past decade have brought British university libraries to this crossroads, and their future depends on their ability to respond to these challenges.

Index

Adlib system 128
academic departments, library budgeting and 29-30
alumni associations, fund raising and 36
Atkinson Report 112-113,168
audiovisual collections 91-92
AUT (Association of University Teachers) 17,49-50

BCOP (Birmingham Libraries in Co-operation) 153,157
binding 92-93
Blackwell index 71,73-74,75,78,79
BLAISE (British Library Automated Information Service) 109,120,124, 126,155,161
BLCMP (Birmingham Libraries Co-operative Mechanization Project) 109,120,124-126,128,129,155, 160-161
Bodleian Library
 automation 135-136
 book selection 82
 budget 26,28,29
 collection expenditure 78
 cooperation within system 155
 copyright deposit 91
 Faculty Library Committee 25
 fund raising 35
 library hours 97
 staff 46,58,65,66
books
 cash expenditure 71,74,76-78
 sales 35
 selection 82-84
 shelving 115
British Library 81
 cooperative activities 153,155-156
 Document Supply Centre 110,156,159
 grants to other libraries 36,55
 Joint Academic Network and 161
 See also BLAISE, LOCAS
British Library of Political and Economic Science 158
BRS system
 See BLCMP
Brunel University
 automation 122
 collection growth rate 69
 fund raising 36
 inter-library loans 110
 library noise control 115

CEEFAX service 105
Centre for Interfirm Comparison 38
CIRCO system 125
City University
 automation 127-128,132
 audiovisual collections 91
 book expenditure 70
 book selection 83
 budget 27
 library management teams 64
 loans 106
 ownership of companies 14
 reorganization 11
CLAIM index 71,76,77,78
CLSI circulation system 108,127-128,132
Computer Board for the Universities and Research Councils 131
computing centres, library automation and 138-141
Conspectus 82,156,158-159
contract research 32
Co-operative Automation Group 161
Copyright Licensing Agency 112
Coventry Polytechnic, cooperative staff training at 157

173

Creswick, H. R. 150
Croham Report 8,18
CURL (Consortium of University Research Libraries) 123,144-145,147, 152-153,161
CVCP (Committee of Vice-Chancellors and Principals) 6-7,10,12,15,38-39,166

Data Protection Act 106
Dobis-Libis system 108,128
Dynix system 123,128

fines, as source of library income 33-34

Geac circulation system 35,83,123-124, 127,128,129,132
Green Paper 6,8-9,10,15-16

HATRICS 153
Heriot-Watt University
  automation 108,127-128
  borrowing rights 157

Index of University Costs 42,70-71,72,73
inter-library loans 34,109-110,156,159
IUCC (Standing Committee of the Inter-University Committee on Computing) 139

JANET (Joint Academic Network) 37,109, 127,132,139,152,155-156,161-162
Jarratt Report 7,10,12-13,15-16,18,24,31, 61,65
Johnson, Paul 11

King's College London
  on-line searching policy 111
  periodical expenditure 79
  staff organization 59

LASER (London and South Eastern Library Region) 159
LIBERTAS system
  See SWALCAP
Librarian (computer system) 128
libraries
  classification 2
  cooperative activities 143-162

enquiry desks 105-106
performance measures 40-41
promotion 102-103,104-105
reduced operating hours 96-97
reorganization 167
users 34-35,98-100
library automation 168-169
  choosing a system 128-132
  computing centres and 138-141
  cooperative activities and 124-125, 135-136,159-162
  effects on library users 137
  effects on staff 136-137
  financial aspects 129-132
  integration 132-134
  library management and 63
  on-line circulation data 106-107
  See also names of specific systems; subhead automation under names of libraries and universities
library budgets 21
  calculation of 26-27
  charging for services 30-31
  cost-centre budgets 28-33
  decline in value 77-80
  one-line budgets 27-28,96,103
  overhead 29
  resource allocation 62-63
  share of university recurrent expenditure 41
  staff expenditure 28,48-50,55-56
library buildings 112-113
  design 114,116-117
  noise levels 115
library catalogues 107
  See also names of specific systems; library automation
library collections
  cash expenditure 70-81,88-90
    See also Blackwell index; CLAIM index
  cooperative activities and 158
  development 90-91
  donations to 91
  mutilation 116
  physical arrangement 114-115
  preservation 93
  rate of growth 69-70

Index

research value 81-82,101-103
transferral to other libraries 87-88
withdrawal of materials 113
Library Committees 21-25
library funding 144
   cuts 40-41,42-43,165-169
   membership fees 34-35
   sales 35
   sources of income 33-38
   See also British Library—grants to other libraries, SCONUL, UGC
library management 24,63-65
   approving new courses 32-33
   planning for the future 170-171
   team approach 56-57,64-66
Library Resources Co-ordinating Committee 158
library security 115-116
library services 100-103
library staff
   communication 65-66
   deputy librarians 55-56
   gender 53
   morale 51-53,65-66
   national grading scheme 49-51
   organizational structure 56-63
   part-time staff 54-55
   subject librarians 59-61,102
   temporary contracts 53-54
   training 66-67,150-151,157
library suppliers 92
LISC (Library and Information Services Council) 144,145,153,162
LOCAS (Local Catalogue Service) 120, 124,156
Loughborough University of Technology
   automation 120,123,133
   budget 32
   interlibrary loans 110
   library building 112
   microcomputer use 133
   Serials Review Group 87

Manpower Services Commission 36-37,55, 109
MARC (Machine-readable cataloguing) 126,127
   See also Library automation

microcomputers, library automation and 133
Moon, Brenda 103
MOYUL (Meeting of Yorkshire University Libraries) 153,157,158

National Health Service, grants to libraries 36
National Library of Scotland 154,159,160
National Library of Wales 154
Northern Regional Library System 159
North Western Regional Library System 159

OCLC (Online Computer Library Center) 109,120,126-127,132
on-line searching 34,110-111
   See also library automation
OPAC (on-line public access catalogue) 107-109,126,127,128,137
   See also library automation
ORACLE service 105
overseas students 14,31-32,100

Pearl system 128
periodicals
   collection assessment 84-88
   expenditure 73-74,75,76
   shelving 115
photocopying, as source of income 33, 111-112
Plymouth Polytechnic 158
PRESTEL service 106

Ratcliffe Report 93
reciprocal rights for readers 157
REMARC (Retrospective Machine-Readable Cataloguing) 109
Robbins Committee 10,13

SASLIC (Surrey and Sussex Librarians in Co-operation) 154
School of Slavonic and East European Studies 158
SCOLCAP (Scottish Libraries Co-operative Automation Project) 124,160
SCONUL (Standing Conference of National and University Libraries) 2,38-40, 81-82,156

Advisory Committee on Automation
  Policy 139
automation funding recommendations
  131
book price indices 71
collection development recommendations
  158-159
collection surveys 69
communication between libraries 156
funding coordination recommendations
  144
funding surveys 32-33,37-38,45,69,119,
  149-150
librarian training recommendations 67,
  150-151
library cooperation recommendations 145
measure of staff expenditure 48-49
operating hour survey 96
structure 146-149
Serials Union List for South Yorkshire 122,
  156-157
Sheffield Plan 18-19
Smethurst, Michael 113
Society of Sussex Librarians 154
South Western Regional Library System
  159
Standing Committee of the Inter-University
  Committee on Computing
  See IUCC
STATUS software 120
S$_3$RBK (Southampton, Surrey, Sussex,
  Reading, Brunel and Kent
  University libraries) 153,158
SWALCAP (South Western Academic
  Libraries Co-operative Automation
  Project) 107,109,120,124-126,128,
  129,132,135,155,160-161

telephone systems, cost control 29
Tobias circulation system 124

UGC (University Grants Committee) 5,10,
  12,15,16,48,71,166
  automation funding 130,131,169
  CURL funding 152
  grant allocations 7-8,11,13-14,32,37,41,
    42,43,78-80
  planning documents 6,18,167
  reorganization proposal 8-9
  resource sharing 143,144
UMIST (University of Manchester Institute
  of Science and Technology)
  automation 128
universities
  commercial activities 14
  financial management 12-14
  funding 6-10
  links with the community 14-15
  planning 6,18-19
  research grants 14
  restructuring 9-13
  standards and accountability 15-16
Universities Academic Salaries Committee
  17
Universities Funding Council 8,167
University College, Cardiff
  collection funding 89
  funding cuts 9
  staff expenditure 47
University College London, budget 26,27
University College of North Wales, Bangor
  automation 126
  funding 8,32
  staff reduction 45
University College of Swansea
  automation 107,125
  cataloguing system 107
  collection growth rate 69
  loans 106,110
University College of Wales, Aberystwyth
  budget 27,32
  circulation system access 107
  inter-library loans 110
university departments, reorganization
  11-12
University of Aberdeen
  automation 122,123,128
  funding 8
  library building 112
  library management teams 64
  on-line searching fees 111
  organizational structure 61
  staff 9,45,46,47,53

storage of materials 113
transferral of collections 88
University of Aston in Birmingham
  automation 126,127,133
  cooperative activities 102
  financial aspects 5,27,32
  Library Committee 24
  library hours 97
  periodical collection 86-87
  promotion 103
  staff organization 57,140
University of Bath
  automation 126
  book sales 35
  cooperative activities 143,145,158
  funding 5,32,88,89
  inter-library loans 110
  Library Liaison Committee 24-25
  on-line searching 111
  photocopying policy 112
  reorganization 10-11
  subject librarians 60
University of Birmingham
  funding 41
  staff 9,47,53,57
University of Bradford
  automation 125
  funding 5,89
  inter-library loans 109-110
  promotion 103
  reorganization 11
  staff 46,48,58
University of Bristol
  cooperative activities 143,158
  staff 46,48,57
University of Buckingham
  automation 128
  collection funding 89
  restructuring 13
  staff contracts 54
University of Cambridge
  automation 123
  book selection 83
  budget 28
  cataloguing system 107,108,109,122-123
  collection expenditure 70,78

  cooperative activities 152,156,158,161
  copyright deposit 91
  funding 5,36
  library membership fee 34
  loans 106
  photocopying policy 112
  staff 47,49,52,58
  student library committee 25
University of Dundee
  automation 127
  collection growth rate 69
  funding 8
  library building 112
University of Durham
  funding 8
  library building 112
  library guides 99
  overseas student fees 32
  student library committee 25
University of East Anglia
  automation 120
  cooperative activities 162
  funding 8
  library management team 64
  periodical collection 86-87
  staff organization 59
University of Edinburgh
  automation 126,132
  borrowing rights 157
  cataloguing system 108
  collection funding 88,89
  computing centre 139,140
  cooperative activities 152
  inter-library loans 110
  library building 113
  Library Committees 23,25
  on-line searching policy 111
  organizational structure 61
  staff 45,46,57
University of Essex, automation 126
University of Exeter
  audiovisual collection 91
  cooperative activities 158,162
  funding 35,41
  library building 112
  on-line circulation system 125

reorganization 11
seminars 25-26
storage of materials 113
University of Glasgow
  automation 126
  cooperative activities 145,152
  fund raising 36
  library building 112,114
  organizational structure 61
  student librarians 59
  transferral of collections 88
University of Hull
  automation 123
  book sales 35
  cataloguing system 108-109
  circulation system 106,107-108,127
  collection expenditure 41,70,79,80
  cooperative activities 154
  funding 37,89
  inter-library loans 109-110
  library buildings 113
  reorganization 11
  staff expenditure 47,48
University of Keele
  budget 27
  funding 5,8
  lack of automation 119
  periodical expenditure 79
University of Kent at Canterbury
  audiovisual collection 91
  automation 122,123,126
  collection growth rate 70
  inter-library loans 110
  library planning 62
  Library Users Group 25
  staff 54,58,134
University of Lancaster
  automation 119,120-121
  circulation system access 107-108
  collection management 87-88
  on-line searching fee 111
University of Leeds
  automation 126
  book expenditure 70
  committees 23-24
  cooperative activities 152

photocopying policy 112
staff cuts 9
University of Leicester, staff cuts 46
University of Liverpool
  automation 108,128
  book expenditure 70
  collection funding 87,89
  Library Committees 23,25
University of London
  automation 135
  book sales 35
  budget 29
  cooperative activities 152,154-155,156, 158
  EUCLID cataloguing system 107
  library fees 34
  LOCAS use 124
  reciprocal rights for readers 157
University of Manchester
  circulation system 108,124
  cooperative activities 152
  inter-library loans 110
  security system 116
  staff mobility 52
University of Newcastle-upon-Tyne
  audiovisual collection 92
  automation 119-120,123,126,134
  budget 27
  cataloguing system 108
  collection expenditure 70,71,73-77
  inter-library loan fee 34
  library building 112,116
  Library Committee 24
  library planning 62
  promotion 99
  staff 46,48,50,60,63,134
University of Nottingham
  book expenditure 70
  fund raising 36
  staff 137
University of Oxford
  automation 122,126,128,129,132
  book expenditure 70
  cooperative activities 152,156,158,161
  photocopying policy 112
  staff 9,13,49

University of Reading
  budget 30
  cataloguing system 107
  collection expenditure 70,71-72,73-77, 78,79
  collection growth rate 69
  cooperative activities 157
  endowment fund 36
  Faculty Library Committee 25
  library building 112,114
  library security 115-116
  on-line circulation system 125
  staff 47,53,57-63
  student library committee 25
University of St. Andrews
  automation 107,120
  cataloguing service use 124
  classmark searches 108
  collection growth rate 69
  funding 34,36,89
  staff expenditure 48
University of Salford
  collection expenditure 71-72,73-77
  computing centre, 139,140
  cooperative activities 162
  funding 5,32
  on-line searching fees 111
  promotion 35,103
  staff 64,140
University of Sheffield
  automation 122
  budget 27
  cataloguing system 107
  Centre for Research and User Studies 2
  company ownership 14
  Library Committee 23
  library tours 25
  reorganization 11
  staff 9,16,46,64
University of Southampton
  automation 119-120,139
  collection development 78,89,91
  cooperative activities 157
  inter-library loans 110
  library building 112,114
  library management team 56
  planning 62
  policy statements 82
  security system 116
  staff 9-13,46,59,60
University of Stirling
  automation 128
  book expenditure 70
  cooperative activities 145
  Library Users Group 25
  staff reduction 46
University of Strathclyde, cataloguing 126
University of Surrey
  automation 121
  funding 41
  periodical expenditure 78
  staff 50,53,65,67
University of Sussex
  audiovisual collections 91
  automation 123-124,127
  budget 29,32,41
  classmark searches 108
  collecting policy 83-84
  collection expenditure 80
  cooperative activities 154
  funding 35,37
  inter-library loans 110
  library groups 25
  on-line searching fees 111
  periodicals collection 79,86-87
  planning committee 24
  staff 50,51,53,54,57,59,140
University of Wales, cooperative activities 154
University of Warwick
  automation 125
  Business Information Service 55,104
  cooperative activities 157
  funding 8
University of York
  automation 120,121,123
  cataloguing system 109
  funding 5,8
  Library Committee 23
  promotion 99
university staff
  age profiles 16-17

salaries 17
tenure 16
See also subhead staff under names of libraries and universities
university students, forecasting numbers 17-18
URICA system 128,132,135
UWIST (University of Wales Institute of Science and Technology)
  automation 125
  budget 31,32,103
  circulation system access 107
  collection funding 88,90
  inter-library loans 110
  on-line searching policy 111
  staff 55,65

Veaner, Allen 21
Videotex services 105-106
Viscount Project 159-160

Westfield College, staff 140
White Paper 8-9,10,13-14,15,18
Wolfson Foundation 152
Working Group on Library Cooperation 154

For Product Safety Concerns and Information please contact our EU
representative GPSR@taylorandfrancis.com
Taylor & Francis Verlag GmbH, Kaufingerstraße 24, 80331 München, Germany

www.ingramcontent.com/pod-product-compliance
Lightning Source LLC
Chambersburg PA
CBHW052122300426
44116CB00010B/1768